Discourse in Machine Translation

(DiscoMT 2013)

Sofia, Bulgaria
9 August 2013

ISBN: 978-1-62993-005-3

Printed from e-media with permission by:

Curran Associates, Inc.
57 Morehouse Lane
Red Hook, NY 12571

Some format issues inherent in the e-media version may also appear in this print version.

Printed by Curran Associates, Inc. (2013)

Association for Computational Linguistics
209 N. Eighth Street
Stroudsburg, Pennsylvania 18360

Phone: 1-570-476-8006
Fax: 1-570-476-0860

acl@aclweb.org

Additional copies of this publication are available from:

Curran Associates, Inc.
57 Morehouse Lane
Red Hook, NY 12571 USA
Phone: 845-758-0400
Fax: 845-758-2634
Email: curran@proceedings.com
Web: www.proceedings.com

DiscoMT 2013

Discourse in Machine Translation

Proceedings of the Workshop

August 9, 2013
Sofia, Bulgaria

Introduction

It is a truism that texts have properties that go beyond those of their individual sentences, including:

- document-wide properties, such as topic mix, style, register, reading level and genre, all of which are manifest in the frequency and distribution of words, word senses, referential forms and syntactic structures;
- patterns of topical or functional sub-structure that show up in localized differences in the frequency and distribution of these elements within documents;
- patterns of discourse coherence, manifest in explicit and implicit relations between sentences (clauses), or between sentences (clauses) and referring forms, or between referring forms themselves;
- common use of reduced expressions that rely on context to convey a lot of information in very few words.

These properties stimulated a good deal of Machine Translation research in the 1990s, aimed at endowing machine–translated target texts with the same document and discourse properties as their source texts, albeit realized differently in source and target languages. This included work on stylistics for Machine Translation (DiMarco & Mah 1994), target language realization of source-language discourse relations (Mitkov 1993) and of referring forms (Bond & Ogura 1998; More et al. 1999; Wada 1990), anaphora resolution for generating appropriate target-language pronouns (Chan and T'sou 1999; Ferrández et al. 1999; Nakaiwa & Ikehara 1992; Nakaiwa 1999), and ellipsis resolution for generating appropriate target-language forms from ellipsed verb-phrases (Balkan 1998). Pointers to much of this work can be found in the *Machine Translation Archive* of conference and workshop papers from the 1990s (see www.mt-archive.info/srch/ling-90.htm).

This early period essentially ended with the 1999 publication of a special issue of the journal *Machine Translation*, edited by Ruslan Mitkov, devoted to anaphora resolution in Machine Translation and multilingual NLP. Only in the past 3–4 years has there been renewed interest in these topics, now from the perspectives of Statistical Machine Translation and Hybrid Machine Translation (Chung & Gildea 2010; Eidelman et al. 2012; Foster et al. 2012; Gong et al. 2011; Guillou 2012; Hardmeier & Federico 2010; Hardmeier et al. 2012; Le Nagard & Koehn 2010; Meyer 2012; Meyer et al. 2012; Voigt & Jurafsky 2012).

With this renewed interest, this ACL Workshop on Discourse in Machine Translation provides a timely forum for the presentation of new approaches to enabling modern systems to produce texts that are not merely sequences of isolated sentences.

Eight submissions have been accepted for the Workshop, on topics that range from multilingual modeling of discourse for machine translation, to actual use of discourse-level features to improve machine translation. From the modeling perspective, the papers presented at the Workshop discuss discourse phenomena such as lexical consistency (Guillou, this volume), lexical cohesion (Beigman Klebanov & Flor, this volume) and implicit connectives (Meyer & Webber, this volume), and "meaning units" with cognitive relevance (Williams et al., this volume). From the perspective of the application to MT, several papers present encouraging results showing that discourse-related features bring measurable improvements to the quality of machine-translated texts. One study uses oracle features, namely connective labels (Meyer & Poláková, this volume), while others use automatically-assigned ones. For instance, the translation of tensed verbs is improved by recognizing whether or not they are conveying narrative material (Meyer et al., this volume); the translation of the pronoun "it" is improved based on lexical, syntactic and anaphoric features (Novák et al., this volume); and a document-level decoder is used when tuning an SMT system, with a sample of readability-related features (Stymne et al., this volume).

The studies presented at the Workshop provide quantitative data and benchmark scores to which future progress on these tasks should be compared. We hope that the Workshop will stimulate further work in these areas, as well as in the many areas of discourse and Machine Translation that are not yet represented.

We would like to thank all the authors who submitted papers to the Workshop, as well as all the members of the Program Committee who reviewed the submissions and delivered thoughtful, informative reviews.

Bonnie Webber (chair), Katja Markert, Andrei Popescu-Belis, Jörg Tiedemann (co-chairs)

References

Lorna Balkan (1998). *A Treatment of Verb Phrase Ellipsis for Machine Translation.* PhD thesis, University of Essex.

Beata Beigman Klebanov and Michael Flor (2013). Associative Texture Is Lost In Translation. *This volume.*

Francis Bond and Kentaro Ogura (1998). Reference in Japanese-English Machine Translation. *Machine Translation*, 13:2-3, pp. 107–134.

Marine Carpuat and Michel Simard (2012). The Trouble with SMT Consistency. *Proceedings of the 7th Workshop on Statistical Machine Translation (WMT)*, pp. 442–449.

Samuel Chan and Benjamin T'sou (1999). Semantic Inference for Anaphora Resolution: Toward a Framework in Machine Translation. *Machine Translation*, 14:3-4, pp. 163–190.

Tagyoung Chung and Dan Gildea (2010). Effects of Empty Categories on Machine Translation. *Proceedings of the Conference on Empirical Methods in Natural Language Processing (EMNLP)*, pp. 636–645.

Chrysanne DiMarco and Keith Mah (1994). A Model of Comparative Stylistics for Machine Translation. *Machine Translation*, 9:1, pp. 21–59.

Vladimir Eidelman, Jordan Boyd-Graber and Philip Resnik (2012). Topic Models for Dynamic Translation Model Adaptation. *Proceedings of the 50th Annual Meeting of the Association for Computational Linguistics*, pp. 115–119.

Antonio Ferrández, Manuel Palomar and Lidia Moreno (1999). An Empirical Approach to Spanish Anaphora Resolution. *Machine Translation*, 14:3-4, pp. 191-216.

George Foster, Pierre Isabelle and Roland Kuhn (2010). Translating Structured Documents. *Proceedings of the Conference of the Association for Machine Translation in the Americas (AMTA).*

Anita Gojun (2010). *Null Subjects in Statistical Machine Translation: A Case Study on Aligning English and Italian Verb Phrases with Pronominal subjects.* Diplomarbeit, Institut für Maschinelle Sprachverarbeitung, University of Stuttgart.

Zhengxian Gong, Min Zhang and Guodong Zhou (2011). Cache-based Document-level Statistical Machine Translation. *Proceedings of the Conference on Empirical Methods in Natural Language Processing (EMNLP)*, pp. 909–919.

Liane Guillou (2012). Improving Pronoun Translation for Statistical Machine Translation. *Proceedings of the Student Research Workshop at the 13th Conference of the European Chapter of the ACL*, pp. 1–10.

Liane Guillou (2013). Analysing Lexical Consistency in Translation. *This volume*.

Christian Hardmeier and Marcello Federico (2010). Modeling Pronominal Anaphora in Statistical Machine Translation. *Proceedings of the International Workshop on Spoken Language Translation (IWSLT)*, pp. 283–289.

Christian Hardmeier, Joakim Nivre and Jörg Tiedemann (2012). Document-wide Decoding for Phrase-based Statistical Machine Translation. *Proceedings of the Conference on Empirical Methods in Natural Language Processing (EMNLP)*, pp. 1179–1190.

Ronan Le Nagard and Philipp Koehn (2010). Aiding Pronoun Translation with Co-reference Resolution. *Proceedings of the Workshop on Statistical Machine Translation (WMT)*, pp. 252–261.

Thomas Meyer (2011). Disambiguating Temporal-contrastive Connectives for Machine Translation. *Proceedings of the Student Research Workshop at the 13th Conference of the European Chapter of the ACL*, pp. 46–51.

Thomas Meyer, Andrei Popescu-Belis, Najeh Hajlaoui and Andrea Gesmundo (2012). Machine Translation of Labeled Discourse Connectives. *Proceedings of the Conference of the Association for Machine Translation in the Americas (AMTA)*.

Thomas Meyer, Cristina Grisot and Andrei Popescu-Belis (2013). Detecting Narrativity to Improve English to French Translation of Simple Past Verbs. *This volume*.

Thomas Meyer and Lucie Poláková (2013). Machine Translation with Many Manually Labeled Discourse Connectives. *This volume*.

Thomas Meyer and Bonnie Webber (2013). Implicitation of Discourse Connectives in (Machine) Translation. *This volume*.

Ruslan Mitkov (1993). How Could Rhetorical Relations Be Used in Machine Translation? (And at least Two Open Questions). *Proceedings of the ACL Workshop on Intentionality and Structure in Discourse Relations*, pp.86–89.

Ruslan Mitkov and Johann Haller (1994). Machine Translation, Ten Years on: Discourse Has Yet to Make a Breakthrough. *Proceedings of the International Conference on Machine Translation: Ten Years on*, Cranfield University, England.

Tatsunori Mori, Mamoru Matsuo and Hiroshi Nakawaga (1999). Zero-subject Resolution Using Linguistic Constraints and Defaults: The Case of Japanese Instruction Manuals. *Machine Translation*, 14:3-4, pp. 231-245.

Hiromi Nakaiwa (1999). Automatic Extraction of Rules for Anaphora Resolution of Japanese Zero Pronouns in Japanese-English Machine Translation from Aligned Sentence Pairs. *Machine Translation*, 14:3-4, pp. 247–279.

Hiromi Nakaiwa and Satoru Ikehara (1992). Zero Pronoun Resolution in a Japanese to English Machine Translation System by Using Verbal Semantic Attributes. *Proceedings of the Third Conference on Applied Natural Language Processing (ANLP)*, pp. 201–208.

Michal Novák, Anna Nedoluzhko and Zdenek Zabokrtsky (2013). Translation of "It" in a Deep Syntax Framework. *This volume*.

Sara Stymne, Christian Hardmeier, Jörg Tiedemann and Joakim Nivre (2013). Feature Weight Optimization for Discourse-Level SMT. *This volume*.

Ferhan Ture, Douglas Oard and Philip Resnik (2012). Encouraging Consistent Translation Choices. *Proceedings of the Conference of the North American Chapter of the Association for Computational Linguistics (NAACL)*, pp. 417–426.

Rob Voigt and Dan Jurafsky (2012). Towards a Literary Machine Translation: The Role of Referential Cohesion. *Proceedings of the NAACL-HLT Workshop on Computational Linguistics for Literature*, pp. 18–25.

Hajime Wada (1990). Discourse Processing in MT: Problems in Pronominal Translation. *Proceedings of the 13th International Conference on Computational Linguistics (Coling)*, pp. 73–75.

Jennifer Williams, Rafael Banchs and Haizhou Li (2013). Meaning Unit Segmentation in English and Chinese: a New Approach to Discourse Phenomena. *This volume*.

Organizing Committee

Bonnie Webber, University of Edinburgh (chair)
Ondřej Bojar, Charles University in Prague
Chris Callison-Burch, Johns Hopkins University
Marcello Federico, FBK-IRST, Trento
Pierre Isabelle, National Research Council Canada
Katja Markert, University of Leeds (co-chair)
Andrei Popescu-Belis, Idiap Research Institute, Martigny (co-chair)
Jörg Tiedemann, University of Uppsala (co-chair)

Program Committee

Trevor Cohn, University of Sheffield
George Foster, National Research Council Canada
Dan Gildea, University of Rochester
Liane Guillou, University of Edinburgh
Christian Hardmeier, University of Uppsala
Hitoshi Isahara, Toyohashi University of Technology
Philipp Koehn, University of Edinburgh
Thomas Meyer, Idiap Research Institute, Martigny
Hwee Tou Ng, National University of Singapore
Michal Novák, Charles University in Prague
Maja Popovic, DFKI GmbH, Berlin
Jean Senellart, SYSTRAN, Paris
Lucia Specia, University of Sheffield
Sara Stymne, University of Uppsala
Gregor Thurmair, Linguatec GmbH, Munich
Min Zhang, Institute for Infocomm Research, A*STAR, Singapore
Sandrine Zufferey, Utrecht University

Table of Contents

Meaning Unit Segmentation in English and Chinese: a New Approach to Discourse Phenomena
Jennifer Williams, Rafael Banchs and Haizhou Li 1

Analysing Lexical Consistency in Translation
Liane Guillou 10

Implicitation of Discourse Connectives in (Machine) Translation
Thomas Meyer and Bonnie Webber 19

Associative Texture Is Lost In Translation
Beata Beigman Klebanov and Michael Flor 27

Detecting Narrativity to Improve English to French Translation of Simple Past Verbs
Thomas Meyer, Cristina Grisot and Andrei Popescu-Belis 33

Machine Translation with Many Manually Labeled Discourse Connectives
Thomas Meyer and Lucie Poláková 43

Translation of "It" in a Deep Syntax Framework
Michal Novák, Anna Nedoluzhko and Zdeněk Žabokrtský 51

Feature Weight Optimization for Discourse-Level SMT
Sara Stymne, Christian Hardmeier, Jörg Tiedemann and Joakim Nivre 60

Conference Program

Friday August 9, 2013

9:00 Introduction by the organizers

9:10 First oral presentation session

9:10 *Meaning Unit Segmentation in English and Chinese: a New Approach to Discourse Phenomena*
Jennifer Williams, Rafael Banchs and Haizhou Li

9:30 *Analysing Lexical Consistency in Translation*
Liane Guillou

9:50 *Implicitation of Discourse Connectives in (Machine) Translation*
Thomas Meyer and Bonnie Webber

10:10 *Associative Texture Is Lost In Translation*
Beata Beigman Klebanov and Michael Flor

10:30 Coffee break

11:00 Poster session, jointly with WMT

In addition to posters from the speakers, posters will also be presented for the following papers:

Detecting Narrativity to Improve English to French Translation of Simple Past Verbs
Thomas Meyer, Cristina Grisot and Andrei Popescu-Belis

Machine Translation with Many Manually Labeled Discourse Connectives
Thomas Meyer and Lucie Poláková

12:30 Lunch break

14:00 Second oral presentation session

14:00 *Translation of "It" in a Deep Syntax Framework*
Michal Novák, Anna Nedoluzhko and Zdeněk Žabokrtský

14:20 *Feature Weight Optimization for Discourse-Level SMT*
Sara Stymne, Christian Hardmeier, Jörg Tiedemann and Joakim Nivre

14:40 Closing discussion

15:30 Coffee break, end of the workshop

Meaning Unit Segmentation in English and Chinese: a New Approach to Discourse Phenomena

Jennifer Williams [†1,2], **Rafael Banchs**[2], **and Haizhou Li**[2]

[1]Department of Linguistics, Georgetown University, Washington, D.C., USA
[2]Institute for Infocomm Research, 1 Fusionpolis Way, Singapore
jaw97@georgetown.edu {rembanchs,hli}@i2r.a-star.edu.sg

Abstract

We present a new approach to dialogue processing in terms of "meaning units". In our annotation task, we asked speakers of English and Chinese to mark boundaries where they could construct the maximal concept using minimal words. We compared English data across genres (news, literature, and policy). We analyzed the agreement for annotators using a state-of-the-art segmentation similarity algorithm and compared annotations with a random baseline. We found that annotators are able to identify meaning units systematically, even though they may disagree on the quantity and position of units. Our analysis includes an examination of phrase structure for annotated units using constituency parses.

1 Introduction

When humans translate and interpret speech in real-time, they naturally segment speech in "minimal sense units" (Oléron & Nanpon, 1965; Benítez & Bajo, 1998) in order to convey the same information from one language to another as though there were a 1-to-1 mapping of concepts between both languages. Further, it is known that people can hold up to 7+/- 2 "chunks" of information in memory at a time by creating and applying meaningful organization schemes to input (Miller, 1956). However, there is no definitive linguistic description for the kind of "meaning units" that human translators create (Signorelli et al., 2011; Hamon et al., 2009; Mima et al., 1998).

The ability to chunk text according to units of meaning is key to developing more sophisticated machine translation (MT) systems that operate in real-time, as well as informing discourse processing and natural language understanding (NLU) (Kolář, 2008). We present an approach to discourse phenomena to address Keller's (2010) call to find a way to incorporate "cognitive plausibility" into natural language processing (NLP) systems. As it has been observed that human translators and interpreters naturally identify a certain kind of "meaning unit" when translating speech in real-time (Oléron & Nanpon, 1965; Benítez & Bajo, 1998), we want to uncover the features of those units in order to automatically identify them in discourse.

This paper presents an experimental approach to annotating meaning units using human annotators from Mechanical Turk. Our goal was to use the results of human judgments to inform us if there are salient features of meaning units in English and Chinese text. We predicted that human-annotated meaning units should systematically correspond to some other linguistic features or combinations of those features (i.e. syntax, phrase boundaries, segments between stop words, etc.). We are interested in the following research questions:

- At what level of granularity do English and Chinese speakers construct meaning units in text?
- Do English and Chinese speakers organize meaning units systematically such that meaning unit segmentations are not random?
- How well do English and Chinese speakers agree on meaning unit boundaries?
- Are there salient syntactic features of meaning units in English and Chinese?
- Can we automatically identify a 1-to-1 mapping of concepts for parallel text, even if there is paraphrasing in one or both languages?

[†] Now affiliated with Massachusetts Institute of Technology Lincoln Laboratory.

While we have not built a chunker or classifier for meaning unit detection, it is our aim that this work will inform how to parse language systematically in a way that is human-understandable. It remains to be seen that automatic tools can be developed to detect meaning units in discourse. Still, we must be informed as to what kinds of chunks are appropriate for humans to allow them to understand information transmitted during translation (Kolář, 2008). Knowledge about meaning units could be important for real-time speech processing, where it is not always obvious where an utterance begins and ends, due to any combination of natural pauses, disfluencies and fillers such as "like, um..". We believe this work is a step towards creating ultra-fast human-understandable simultaneous translation systems that can be used for conversations in different languages.

This paper is organized as follows: Section 2 discusses related work, Section 3 describes the segmentation similarity metric that we used for measuring annotator agreement, Section 4 describes our experiment design, Section 5 shows experiment results, Section 6 provides analysis, and Section 7 discusses future work.

2 Related Work

At the current state of the art, automatic simultaneous interpretation systems for speech function too slowly to allow people to conduct normal-paced conversations in different languages. This problem is compounded by the difficulty of identifying meaningful endpoints of utterances before transmitting a translation. For example, there is a perceived lag time for speakers when trying to book flights or order products over the phone. This lag time diminishes conversation quality since it takes too long for each speaker to receive a translation at either end of the system (Paulik et al., 2009). If we can develop a method to automatically identify segments of meaning as they are spoken, then we could significantly reduce the perceived lag time in real-time speech-to-speech translation systems and improve conversation quality (Baobao et al., 2002; Hamon et al., 2009).

The problem of absence of correspondence arises when there is a lexical unit (single words or groups of words) that occurs in L1 but not in L2 (Lambert et al., 2005). It happens when words belonging to a concept do not correspond to phrases that can be aligned in both languages. This problem is most seen when translating speech-to-speech in real-time. One way to solve this problem is to identify units for translation that correspond to concepts. A kind of meaning unit had been previously proposed as *information units* (IU), which would need to be richer than semantic roles and also be able to adjust when a mistake or assumption is realized (Mima et al., 1998). These units could be used to reduce the explosion of unresolved structural ambiguity which happens when ambiguity is inherited by a higher level syntactic structure, similar to the use of constituent boundaries for transfer-driven machine translation (TDMT) (Furuse et al., 1996).

The human ability to construct concepts involves both bottom-up and top-down strategies in the brain. These two kinds of processes interact and form the basis of comprehension (Kintsch, 2005). The construction-integration model (CI-2) describes how meaning is constructed from both long-term memory and short-term memory. One of the challenges of modeling meaning is that it requires a kind of *world-knowledge* or *situational knowledge*, in addition to knowing the meanings of individual words and knowing how words can be combined. Meaning is therefore constructed from long-term memory – as can be modeled by latent semantic analysis (LSA) – but also from short-term memory which people use *in the moment* (Kintsch & Mangalath, 2011). In our work, we are asking annotators to construct meaning from well-formed text and annotate where units of meaning begin and end.

3 Similarity Agreement

We implemented *segmentation similarity* (S) from Fournier and Inkpen (2012). Segmentation similarity was formulated to address some gaps of the *WindowDiff* (WD) metric, including unequal penalty for errors as well as the need to add padding to the ends of each segmentation (Pevzner & Hearst, 2002). There are 3 types of segmentation errors for (S), listed below:

1. s_1 contains a boundary that is off by n potential boundaries in s_2
2. s_1 contains a boundary that s_2 does not, or
3. s_2 contains a boundary that s_1 does not

These three types of errors are understood as *transpositions* in the case of error type 1, and as *substitutions* in the case of error types 2 and 3. Note that there is no distinction between insertions and deletions because neither of the segmentations are considered reference or hypothesis. We show the specification of (S) in (1):

$$S_{(si1,si2)} = \frac{\mathbf{t} \cdot mass(i) - \mathbf{t} - d_{(si1,si2,T)}}{\mathbf{t} \cdot mass(i) - \mathbf{t}} \quad (1)$$

such that S scales the cardinality of the set of boundary types **t** because the edit distance function $d_{(si1,si2,T)}$ will return a value for potential boundaries of $[0, \mathbf{t} \cdot mass(i)]$ normalized by the number of potential boundaries per boundary type. The value of $mass(i)$ depends on task, in our work we treat mass units as number of words, for English, and number of characters for Chinese. Since our annotators were marking only units of meaning, there was only one boundary type, and $(\mathbf{t} = 1)$. The distance function $d_{(si1,si2,T)}$ is the edit distance between segments calculated as the number of boundaries involved in transposition operations subtracted from the number of substitution operations that could occur. A score of 1.0 indicates full agreement whereas a score of 0 indicates no agreement.

In their analysis and comparison of this new metric, Fournier and Inkpen (2012) demonstrated the advantages of using (S) over using (WD) for different kinds of segmentation cases such as maximal/minimal segmentation, full misses, near misses, and segmentation mass scale effects. They found that in each of these cases (S) was more stable than (WD) over a range of segment sizes. That is, when considering different kinds of misses (false-positive, false-negative, and both), the metric (S) is less variable to internal segment size. These are all indications that (S) is a more reliable metric than (WD).

Further, (S) properly takes into account chance agreement - called *coder bias* - which arises in segmentation tasks when human annotators either decide not to place a boundary at all, or are unsure if a boundary should be placed. Fournier and Inkpen (2012) showed that metrics that follow (S) specification reflect most accurately on coder bias, when compared to mean pairwise $1 - WD$ metrics. Therefore we have decided to use segmentation similarity as a metric for annotator agreement.

4 Experiment Design

This section describes how we administered our experiment as an annotation task. We surveyed participants using Mechanical Turk and presented participants with either English or Chinese text. While the ultimate goal of this research direction is to obtain meaning unit annotations for speech, or transcribed speech, we have used well-structured text in our experiment in order to find out more about the potential features of meaning units in the simplest case.

4.1 Sample Text Preparation

Genre: Our text data was selected from three different genres for English (news, literature, and policy) and one genre for Chinese (policy). We used 10 articles from the Universal Declaration of Human Rights (UDHR) in parallel for English and Chinese. The English news data (NEWS) consisted of 10 paragraphs that were selected online from www.cnn.com and reflected current events from within the United States. The English literature data (LIT) consisted of 10 paragraphs from the novel Tom Sawyer by Mark Twain. The English and Chinese UDHR data consisted of 12 parallel paragraphs from the Universal Declaration of Human Rights. The number of words and number of sentences by language and genre is presented below in Table 1.

Preprocessing: To prepare the text samples for annotation, we did some preprocessing. We removed periods and commas in both languages, since these markings can give structure and meaning to the text which could influence annotator decisions about meaning unit boundaries. For the English data, we did not fold to lowercase and we acknowledge that this was a design oversight. The Chinese text was automatically segmented into words before the task using ICTCLAS (Zhang et al., 2003). This was done in order to encourage Chinese speakers to look beyond the character-level and word-level, since word segmentation is a well-known NLP task for the Chinese language. The Chinese UDHR data consisted of 856 characters. We placed checkboxes between each word in the text.

4.2 Mechanical Turk Annotation

We employed annotators using Amazon Mechanical Turk Human Intelligence Tasks (HITs). All instructions for the task were presented in En-

Language and Genre	# words	# Sentences
Chinese UDHR	485	20
English NEWS	580	20
English LIT	542	27
English UDHR	586	20

Table 1: Number of words and sentences by language and genre.

glish. Each participant was presented with a set of numbered paragraphs with a check-box between each word where a boundary could possibly exist. In the instructions, participants were asked to check the boxes between words corresponding to the boundaries of meaning units. They were instructed to create units of meaning larger than words but that are also the "maximal concept that you can construct that has the minimal set of words that can be related to each individual concept"[1]. We did not provide marked examples to the annotators so as to avoid influencing their annotation decisions.

Participants were given a maximum of 40 minutes to complete the survey and were paid USD $1.00 for their participation. As per Amazon Mechanical Turk policy, each of the participants were at least 18 years of age. The annotation task was restricted to one task per participant, in other words if a participant completed the English NEWS annotation task then they could not participate in the Chinese UDHR task, etc. We did not test any of the annotators for language aptitude or ability, and we did not survey language background. It is possible that for some annotators, English and Chinese were not a native language.

5 Results

We omitted survey responses for which participants marked less than 30 boundaries total, as well as participants who completed the task in less than 5 minutes. We did this in an effort to eliminate annotator responses that might have involved random marking of the checkboxes, as well as those who marked only one or two checkboxes. We decided it would be implausible that less than 30 boundaries could be constructed, or that the task could be completed in less than 5 minutes, considering that there were several paragraphs and sentences for each dataset. After we removed those responses, we had solicited 47 participants for English NEWS, 40 participants for English LIT, 59 participants for English UDHR, and 10 participants for Chinese UDHR. The authors acknowledge that the limited sample size for Chinese UDHR data does not allow a direct comparison across the two languages, however we have included it in results and analysis as supplemental findings and encourage future work on this task across multiple languages. We are unsure as to why there was a low number of Chinese annotators in this task, except perhaps the task was not as accessible to native Chinese speakers because the task instructions were presented in English.

5.1 Distributions by Genre

We show distributions of number of annotators and number of units identified for each language and genre in Figures 1 – 4. For each of the language/genres, we removed one annotator because the number of units that they found was greater than 250, which we considered to be an outlier in our data. We used the Shapiro-Wilk Test for normality to determine which, if any, of these distributions were normally distributed. We failed to reject the null hypothesis for Chinese UDHR ($p = 0.373$) and English NEWS ($p = 0.118$), and we rejected the null hypothesis for English LIT ($p = 1.8X10^{-04}$) and English UDHR ($p = 1.39X10^{-05}$).

Dataset	N	Avg Units	Avg Words/Unit
Chinese UDHR	9	70.1	–
English NEWS	46	84.9	6.8
English LIT	39	85.4	6.3
English LIT G1	26	66.9	8.1
English LIT G2	13	129.0	4.2
English UDHR	58	90.1	6.5
English UDHR G1	17	52.2	11.2
English UDHR G2	19	77.3	7.6
English UDHR G3	22	132.2	4.4

Table 2: Number of annotators (N), average number of units identified, average number of words per unit identified, by language and genre.

Since the number of units were not normally distributed for English LIT and English UDHR,

[1]The definition of "meaning units" we provide is very ambiguous and can justify for different people understanding the task differently. However, this is part of what we wanted to measure, as giving a more precise and operational definition would bias people to some specific segmentation criteria.

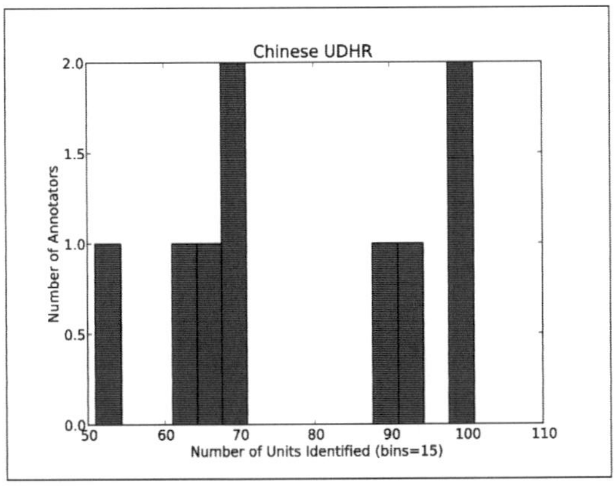

Figure 1: Distribution of total number of annotations per annotator for Chinese UDHR.

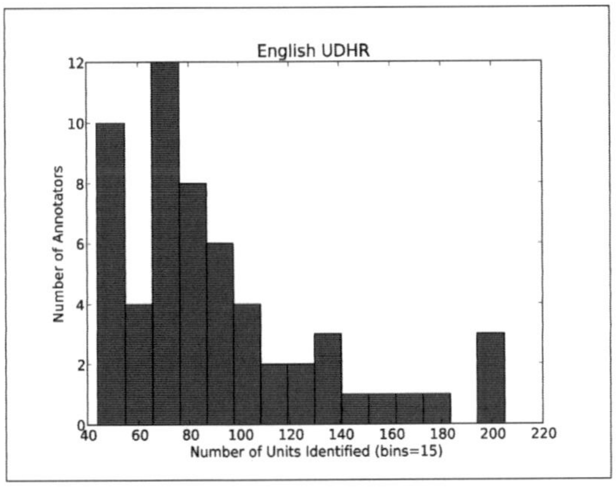

Figure 2: Distribution of total number of annotations per annotator for English UDHR.

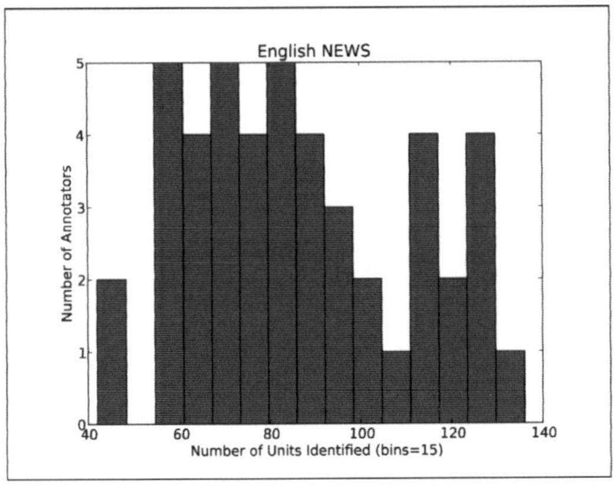

Figure 3: Distribution of total number of annotations per annotator for English NEWS.

we used 2-sample Kolmogorov-Smirnov (KS) Tests to identify separate distributions for each of these genres. We found 3 distinct groups in English UDHR (G1–G3) and 2 distinct groups in English LIT (G1 and G2). Table 2 provides more

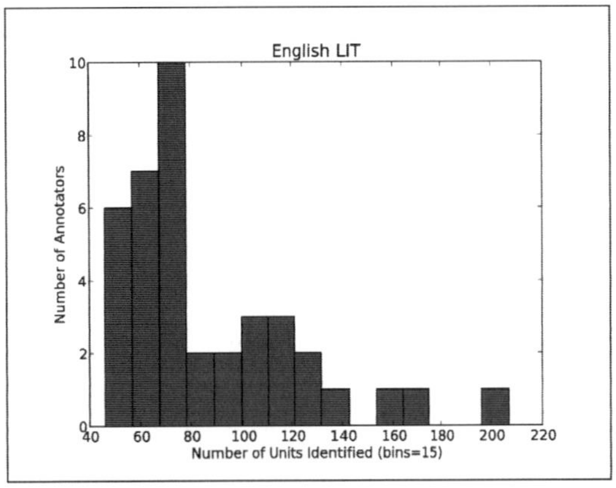

Figure 4: Distribution of total number of annotations per annotator for English LIT.

detailed information about distributions for number of annotations, as well as the average number of units found, and average words per unit. This information informs us as to how large or small on average the meaning units are. Note that in Table 2 we include information for overall English UDHR and overall English LIT distributions for reference. The authors found it interesting that, from Table 2, the number of words per meaning unit generally followed the 7 +/- 2 "chunks" phenomenon, where chunks are words.

5.2 Annotator Agreement

Even though some of the annotators agreed about the number of units, that does not imply that they agreed on where the boundaries were placed. We used segmentation similarity (S) as a metric for annotator agreement. The algorithm requires specifying a unit of measurement between boundaries – in our case we used word-level units for English data and character-level units for Chinese data. We calculated average similarity agreement for segment boundaries pair-wise within-group for annotators from each of the 9 language/genre datasets, as presented in Table 3.

While the segmentation similarity agreements seem to indicate high annotator agreement, we wanted to find out if that agreement was better than what we could generate at random, so we compared annotator agreement with random baselines. To generate the baselines, we used the average number of segments per paragraph in each language/genre dataset and inserted boundaries at random. For each of the 9 language/genre datasets, we generated 30 baseline samples. We calculated the baseline segmentation similarity

Dataset	(S)	(SBL)
Chinese UDHR	**0.930**	0.848
English NEWS	**0.891**	0.796
English LIT	**0.875**	0.790
English LIT G1	**0.929**	0.824
English LIT G2	**0.799**	0.727
English UDHR	**0.870**	0.802
English UDHR G1	**0.929**	0.848
English UDHR G2	**0.910**	0.836
English UDHR G3	**0.826**	0.742

Table 3: Within-group segmentation similarity agreement (S) and segmentation similarity agreement for random baseline (SBL).

(SBL) in the same way using average pair-wise agreement within-group for all of the baseline datasets, shown in Table 3.

For English UDHR, we also calculated average pair-wise agreement across groups, shown in Table 4. For example, we compared English UDHR G1 with English UDHR G2, etc. Human annotators consistently outperformed the baseline across groups for English UDHR.

Dataset	(S)	(SBL)
English UDHR G1–G2	**0.916**	0.847
English UDHR G1–G3	**0.853**	0.782
English UDHR G2–G3	**0.857**	0.778

Table 4: English UDHR across-group segmentation similarity agreement (S) and random baseline (SBL).

6 Analysis

Constructing concepts in this task is systematic as was shown from the segmentation similarity scores. Since we know that the annotators agreed on some things, it is important to find out what they have agreed on. In our analysis, we examined unit boundary locations across genres in addition to phrase structure using constituency parses. In this section, we begin to address another of our original research questions regarding how well speakers agree on meaning unit boundary positions across genres and which syntactic features are the most salient for meaning units.

6.1 Unit Boundary Positions for Genres

Boundary positions are interesting because they can potentially indicate if there are salient parts of the texts which stand out to annotators across genres. We have focused this analysis across genres for the overall data for each of the 4 language/genre pairs. Therefore, we have omitted the subgroups – English UDHR groups (G1,G2, G3) and English LIT groups (G1, G2). Although segmentation similarity is greater within-group from Table 3, this was not enough to inform us of which boundaries annotators fully agree on. For each of the datasets, we counted the number of annotators who agreed on a given boundary location and plotted histograms. In these plots we show the number of annotators of each potential boundary between words. We show the resulting distributions in Figures 5 – 8.

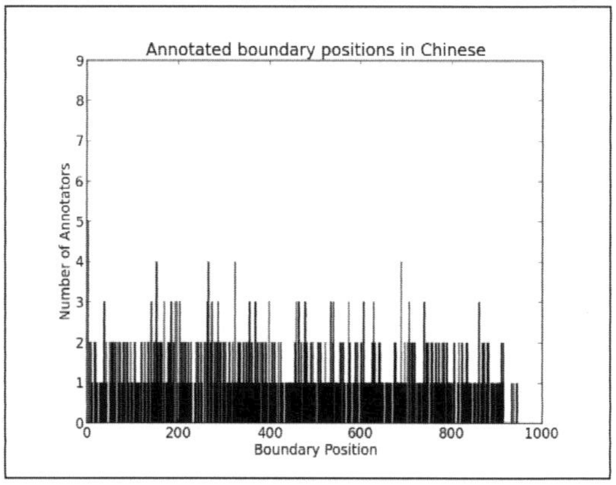

Figure 5: Annotated boundary positions Chinese UDHR.

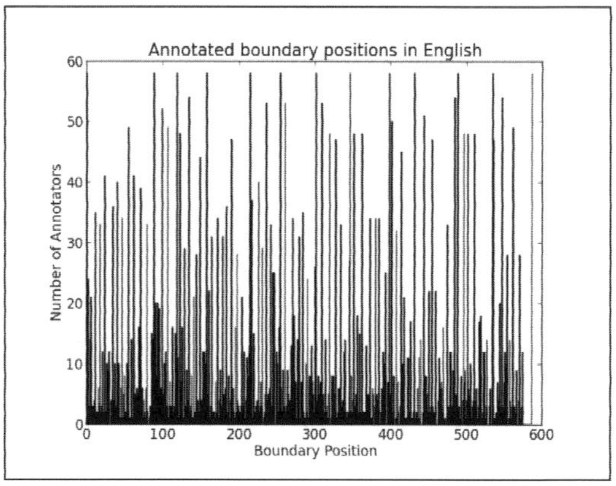

Figure 6: Annotated boundary positions English UDHR.

While there were not many annotators for the Chinese UDHR data, we can see from Figure 5

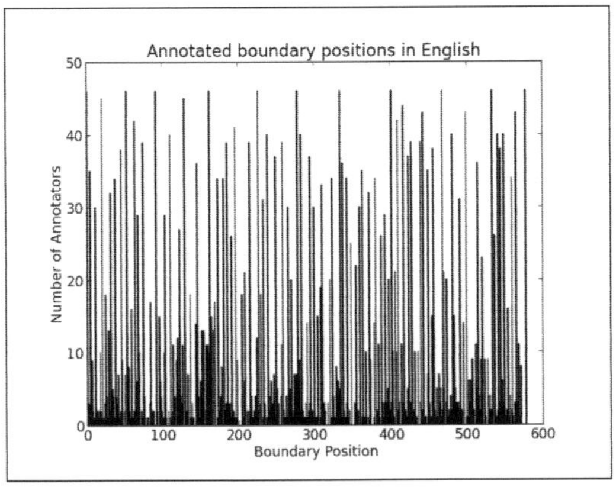

Figure 7: Annotated boundary positions English NEWS.

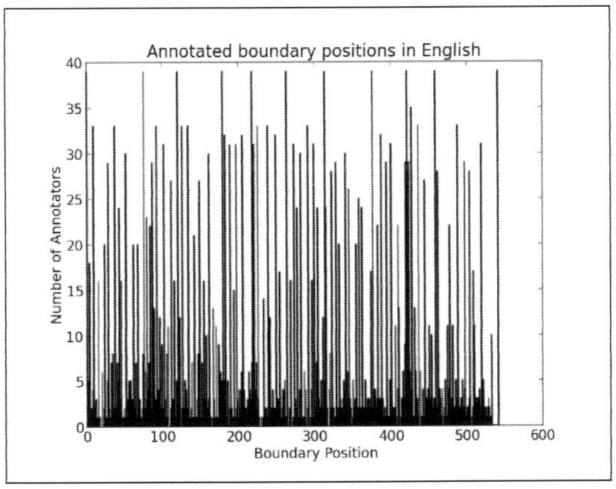

Figure 8: Annotated boundary positions English LIT.

that at most 4 annotators agreed on boundary positions. We can see from Figures 6 – 8 that there is high frequency of agreement in the text which corresponds to paragraph boundaries for the English data, however paragraph boundaries were artificially introduced into the experiment because each paragraph was numbered.

Since we had removed all punctuation markings, including periods and commas for both languages, it is interesting to note there was not full agreement about sentence boundaries. While we did not ask annotators to mark sentence boundaries, we hoped that these would be picked up by the annotators when they were constructing meaning units in the text. Only 3 sentence boundaries were identified by at most 2 Chinese UDHR annotators. On the other hand, all of the sentence boundaries were idenfied for English UDHR and English NEWS, and one sentence boundary was unmarked for English LIT. However, there were no sentence boundaries in the English data that were marked by all annotators - in fact the single most heavily annotated sentence boundary was for English NEWS, where 30% of the annotators marked it. The lack for identifying sentence boundaries could be due to an oversight by annotators, or it could also be indicative of the difficulty and ambiguity of the task.

6.2 Phrase Structure

To answer our question of whether or not there are salient syntactic features for meaning units, we did some analysis with constituency phrase structure and looked at the maximal projections of meaning units. For each of the 3 English genres (UDHR, NEWS, and LIT) we identified boundaries where at least 50% of the annotators agreed. For the Chinese UDHR data, we identified boundaries where at least 30% of annotators agreed. We used the Stanford PCFG Parser on the original English and Chinese text to obtain constituency parses (Klein & Manning, 2003), then aligned the agreeable segment boundaries with the constituency parses. We found the maximal projection corresponding to each annotated unit and we calculated the frequency of each of the maximal projections. The frequencies of part-of-speech for maximal projections are shown in Tables 5 - 8. Note that the part-of-speech tags reflected here come from the Stanford PCFG Parser.

Max. Projection	**Description**	**Freq.**
S, SBAR, SINV	Clause	28
PP	Prepositional Phrase	14
VP	Verb Phrase	11
NP	Noun Phrase	5
ADJP	Adjective Phrase	3
ADVP	Adverb Phrase	1

Table 5: Frequency of maximal projections for English UDHR, for 62 boundaries.

Max. Projection	**Description**	**Freq.**
S, SBAR, SINV	Clause	30
VP	Verb Phrase	23
NP	Noun Phrase	11
PP	Prepositional Phrase	3
ADVP	Adverb Phrase	2

Table 6: Frequency of maximal projections for English NEWS, for 69 boundaries.

Max. Projection	Description	Freq.
S, SBAR	Clause	32
VP	Verb Phrase	10
NP	Noun Phrase	3
PP	Prepositional Phrase	2
ADVP	Adverb Phrase	2

Table 7: Frequency of maximal projections for English LIT, for 49 boundaries.

Max. Projection	Description	Freq.
NN, NR	Noun	22
VP	Verb Phrase	8
NP	Noun Phrase	8
CD	Determiner	3
ADVP	Adverb Phrase	1
AD	Adverb	1
VV	Verb	1
JJ	Other noun mod.	1
DP	Determiner Phrase	1

Table 8: Frequency of maximal projections for Chinese UDHR, for 46 boundaries.

Clauses were by far the most salient boundaries for annotators of English. On the other hand, nouns, noun phrases, and verb phrases were the most frequent for annotators of Chinese. There is some variation across genres for English. This analysis begins to address whether or not it is possible to identify syntactic features of meaning units, however it leaves open another question as to if it is possible to automatically identify a 1-to-1 mapping of concepts across languages.

7 Discussion and Future Work

We have presented an experimental framework for examining how English and Chinese speakers make meaning out of text by asking them to label places that they could construct concepts with as few words as possible. Our results show that there is not a unique "meaning unit" segmentation criteria among annotators. However, there seems to be some preferential trends on how to perform this task, which suggest that any random segmentation is not acceptable. As we have simplified the task of meaning unit identification by using well-structured text from the Universal Declaration of Human Rights, news, and literature, future work should examine identifying meaning units in transcribed speech.

Annotators for the English UDHR and English LIT datasets could be characterized by their different granularities of annotation in terms of number of units identified. These observations are insightful to our first question: what granularity do people use to construct meaning units? For some, meaning units consist of just a few words, whereas for others they consist of longer phrases or possibly clauses. As we did not have enough responses for the Chinese UDHR data, we are unable to comment if identification of meaning units in Chinese fit a similar distribution as with English and we leave in-depth cross-language analysis to future work.

A particularly interesting finding was that human annotators share agreement even across groups, as seen from Table 4. This means that although annotators may not agree on the number of meaning units found, they do share some agreement regarding where in the text they are creating the meaning units. These findings seem to indicate that annotators are creating meaning units systematically regardless of granularity.

Our findings suggest that different people organize and process information differently. This is a very important conclusion for discourse analysis, machine translation and many other applications as this suggests that there is no optimal solution to the segmentation problems considered in these tasks. Future research should focus on better understanding the trends we identified and the observed differences among different genres. While we did not solicit feedback from annotators in this experiment, we believe that it will be important to do so in future work to improve the annotation task. We know that the perceived lag time in speech-to-speech translation cannot be completely eliminated but we are interested in systems that are "fast" enough for humans to have quality conversations in different languages.

Acknowledgments

This work was partly supported by Singapore Agency for Science, Technology and Research (A-STAR) and the Singapore International Pre-Graduate Award (SIPGA) and was partly supported by the National Science Foundation (NSF) award IIS-1225629. Any opinions expressed in this material are those of the authors and do not necessarily reflect the views of A-STAR and NSF.

References

Chang Baobao, Pernilla Danielsson, and Wolfgang Teubert. 2002. Extraction of translation units from Chinese-English parallel corpora. In *Proceedings of the first SIGHAN workshop on Chinese language processing - Volume 18 (SIGHAN '02)*, 1–5.

Presentación Padilla Benítez and Teresa Bajo. 1998. Hacia un modelo de memoria y atención en interpretación simultánea. *Quaderns. Revista de traducció*, 2:107–117.

Chris Fournier and Diana Inkpen. 2012. Segmentation and similarity agreement. In *Proceedings of the 2012 Conference of the North American Chapter of the Association for Computational Linguistics: Human Language Technologies (NAACL HLT '12)*, Montreal, Canada, 152–161.

Osamu Furuse and Hitashi Iida. 1996. Incremental translation utilizing constituent boundary patterns. In *Proceedings of the 16th conference on Computational linguistics (COLING '96)*, Copenhagen, Denmark, 412–417.

Olivier Hamon, Christian Fgen, Djamel Mostefa, Victoria Arranz1, Munstin Kolss, Alex Waibel, and Khalid Choukri. 2009. End-to-End Evaluation in Simultaneous Translation. In *Proceedings of the 12th Conference of the European Chapter of the Association for Computational Linguistics, (EACL '09)*, Athens, Greece, 345–353.

Daniel Jurafsky. 1988. Issues in relating syntax and semantics. In *Proceedings of the 12th International conference on Computational Linguistics (COLING '88)*, Budapest, Hungary, 278–284.

Frank Keller. 2010. Cognitively plausible models of human language processing. In *Proceedings of the ACL 2010 Conference Short Papers*, Uppsala, Sweden, 60–67.

Walter Kintsch. 2005. An Overview of Top-down and Bottom–up Effects in Comprehension: The CI Perspective. *Discourse Processes*, 39(2&3):125–128.

Walter Kintsch and Praful Mangalath. 2011. The Construction of Meaning. *Topics in Cognitive Science*, 3:346–370.

Dan Klein and Christopher D. Manning 2003. Accurate Unlexicalized Parsing. In *Proceedings of the 41st Meeting of the Association for Computational Linguistics*, 423–430.

Jáchym Kolář. 2008. *Automatic Segmentation of Speech into Sentence-like Units.* Ph.D. thesis, University of West Bohemia, Pilsen, Czech Republic.

Patrik Lambert, Adrià. De Gispert, Rafael Banchs, and José B. Mariño. 2005. Guidelines for Word Alignment Evaluation and Manual Alignment. *Language Resources and Evaluation (LREC)*, 39:267–285.

Chi-kiu Lo, Anand Karthik Tumuluru, and Dekai Wu. 2012. Fully automatic semantic MT evaluation. In *Proceedings of the Seventh Workshop on Statistical Machine Translation (WMT '12)*, Montreal, Canada 243–252.

George A. Miller. 1956. The Magical Number Seven, Plus or Minus Two: Some Limits on Our Capacity of Processing Information. *The Psychological Review*, Vol 63:81–97.

Hideki Mima, Hitoshi Iida, and Osamu Furuse. 1998. Simultaneous interpretation utilizing example-based incremental transfer. In *Proceedings of the 17th International Conference on Computational Linguistics (COLING '98)* Montreal, Quebec, Canada, 855–861.

Pierre Oléron and Hubert Nanpon. 1965. Recherches sur la traduction simultanée. *Journal de Psychologie Normale et Pathologique*, 62(1):73–94.

Mathais Paulik and Alex Waibel. 2009. Automatic Translation from Parallel Speech: Simultaneous Interpretation as MT Training Data. *IEEE Workshop on Automatic Speech Recognition and Understanding*, Merano, Italy, 496–501.

Lev Pevzner and Marti A. Hearst 2002. A critique and improvement of an evaluation metric for text segmentation. *Computational Linguistics*, 28(1):1936. MIT Press, Cambridge, MA, USA.

Sameer Pradhan, Wayne Ward, Kadri Hacioglu, James H. Mar- tin, and Dan Jurafsky. 2004. Shallow Semantic Parsing Using Support Vector Machines. In *Proceedings of the 2004 Conference on Human Language Technology and the North American Chapter of the Association for Computational Linguistics (HLT-NAACL-04)*.

Baskaran Sankaran, Ajeet Grewal, and Anoop Sarkar. 2010. Incremental Decoding for Phrase-based Statistical Machine Translation. In *Proceedings of the Joint 5th Workshop on Statistical Machine Translation and Metrics (MATR)*, Uppsala, Sweden, 222–229.

Teresa M. Signorelli, Henk J. Haarmann, and Loraine K. Obler. 2011. Working memory in simultaneous interpreters: Effects of task and age. *International Journal of Billingualism*, 16(2): 192–212.

Hua-Ping Zhang, Hong-Kui Yu, De-Yi Xiong, Qun Liu. 2003. HHMM-based Chinese Lexical Analyzer ICTCLAS. In *Proceedings of the Second SIGHAN Workshop on Chinese Language Processing (SIGHAN '03)* - Volume 17, Sapporo, Japan, 184-187.

Analysing Lexical Consistency in Translation

Liane Guillou
School of Informatics
University of Edinburgh
Scotland, United Kingdom
L.K.Guillou@sms.ed.ac.uk

Abstract

A number of approaches have been taken to improve lexical consistency in Statistical Machine Translation. However, little has been written on the subject of where and when to encourage consistency. I present an analysis of human authored translations, focussing on words belonging to different parts-of-speech across a number of different genres.

1 Introduction

Writers are often given mixed messages with respect to word choice. On one hand they are encouraged to vary their use of words (in essay writing): "It is also important that the words you use are varied, so that you aren't using the same words again and again."[1]. On the other hand they are encouraged to use the same words (only changing the determiner) when referring to the same entity a second time (in technical writing): "The first time a single countable noun is introduced, use *a*. Thereafter, when referring to that same item, use *the*." [2].

Halliday and Hassan (1976) showed that well-written documents exhibit lexical cohesion in terms of what they call *reiteration* and *collocation*. Reiteration is achieved via repetition as well as the use of synonyms and hypernyms. A collocation is a sequence of words / terms that co-occur regularly in text. Examples of collocated pairs of words include "fast food", "bright idea" and "nuclear family". Any source language document will therefore contain repeated instances of the same words or *lemmas* (morphological variants of the same words). This repeated use of words and lemmas is known as *lexical consistency* and the instances can be grouped together to form *lexical chains* (Morris and Hirst, 1991). Lexical chains were proposed by Lotfipour-Saedi (1997) as one feature of a text via which translational equivalence between source and target could be measured.

While Statistical Machine Translation (SMT) has gone from ignoring these properties of discourse by translating sentences independently, to trying to impose *lexical consistency* at a universal level, both approaches have given little consideration to what might be standard practice among human translators.

In order to discover what the standard practice might be, and thus what an SMT system might better aim to achieve, I have carried out a detailed analysis of lexical consistency in human translation. For comparison, I also present an analysis of translations produced by an SMT system. I have considered a variety of genres, as genre correlates with the *function* of a text, which in turn predicts its important elements. A preliminary conclusion of this analysis is that human translators use lexical consistency to support what is important in a text.

2 Related Work

2.1 Unique Terms and Lexical Consistency

Intuitively, it seems obvious that specialised, "semantically heavy" words like "genome" and "hypochondria" will only have a single exact translation into any given target language, and as such will tend to be translated with greater consistency than semantically "light" words. Melamed (1997) showed that this intuition could be quantified using the concept of *entropy*, which the

[1] Purdue University, Online Writing Lab: http://owl.english.purdue.edu/engagement/index.php?category_id=2&sub_category_id=2&article_id=66. Accessed 21/04/2013

[2] Monash University, Language and Learning OnLine: http://monash.edu.au/lls/llonline/grammar/engineering/articles/6.xml. Accessed 21/04/2013

author uses over a large corpus to show what words and what parts-of-speech are more likely to be translated consistently than others. However, Melamed's analysis ignores any segmentation of the corpus by document, topic, speaker/writer or translator, considering only overall translational distributions. It is therefore similar to that which can be gleaned from the phrase table in a modern SMT system.

2.2 Enforcing and Encouraging Consistency

A number of approaches have been taken to both encourage and enforce lexical consistency in SMT. These range from the cache-based model approaches of Tiedemann (2010a; 2010b) and Gong et al. (2011), to the post-editing approach of Xiao et al. (2011) and discriminative learning approach of Ma et al. (2011) and He et al. (2011).

Carpuat (2009) and Ture et al. (2012) suggested that the *one sense per discourse* constraint (Gale et al., 1992) might apply as well to *one sense per translation*. Both demonstrated that exploiting this constraint in SMT led to better quality translations. Ture et al. (2012) encourage consistency themselves using soft constraints implemented as additional features in a hierarchical phrase-based translation model.

What has not been adequately addressed in the available MT literature is *where* and *when* lexical consistency is desirable in translation.

2.3 Measuring Consistency

In contrast with *entropy* following from lexical properties of words (i.e. how many senses a word has, and how many different possible ways there are of translating each sense in a given target language), as explored in (Melamed, 1997), Itagaki et al (2007) developed a way to measure the terminological consistency of a *single* document. They define *consistency* as a measure of the number of translation variations for a term and the frequency for each variation. They adapted the Herfindahl-Hirschman Index (HHI) measure, typically used to measure market concentration, to measure the consistency of a single term in a single document. HHI is defined as:

$$HHI = \sum_{i=1}^{n} s_i^2$$

Where *i* ranges over the *n* different ways that the given term has been translated in the document, and s_i is the ratio of the number of times the term has been translated as *i* to the number of times it has been translated. The lower the index, the more variation there is in translation of the term, i.e. the less consistent the translation. The maximum index is 10,000 (or 1 using the normalised scale) for a completely consistent translation.

HHI is best illustrated with examples of distributions over a *single document*. An English word with two French translations that are observed with equal frequency will receive a score of: $0.50^2 + 0.50^2 = 0.5$. A different English word with two French translations observed 80% and 20% of the time will receive a score of: $0.90^2 + 0.10^2 = 0.82$ representing a more consistent translation of the English word. When the number of possible French translations increases, the HHI score will likely decrease unless one translation is much more frequent - see previous example. An English word with three translations observed with equal frequency (33.3% each) will have a score of: $0.33^2 + 0.33^2 + 0.33^2 = 0.33$ representing a word that is translated with lower consistency.

Itagaki et al. incorporate these HHI scores (one score per term, per document) in a wider calculation that measures inter-document consistency of a set of documents that all use the same term. As the analyses presented in this paper are concerned with single documents and their translations, the per term, per document HHI scores are sufficient.

3 Methodology

This section describes analyses of manual (human) translation and automated translation (by a phrase-based SMT system). The data used is described in Section 3.1 and the methods for analysing consistency in human and automated translation are described in Sections 3.2 and 3.3.

3.1 Data

As the focus of the analysis is lexical consistency, it was important to select texts that were written/translated by the same author. The typical corpora used in training SMT systems were dismissed; Europarl as speakers change frequently and news-crawl as the articles are typically too short to exhibit much lexical repetition. Instead I selected the INTERSECT corpus (Salkie, 2010) which contains a collection of sentence-aligned parallel texts from different genres. From this corpus I extracted a number of texts from the English-

Title	Genre	Sentences	Words		En POS Count			Fr POS Count		
			En	Fr	N	A	V	N	A	V
English Source										
Xerox ScanWorx Manual	Instructions	2,573	38,698	44,841	14,060	2,308	6,555	15,206	2,528	8,822
On the Origin of Species	Natural Science	1,702	62,454	68,016	13,774	6,868	9,857	17,452	6,291	12,895
Dracula Ch. 1-2	Novel	584	11,209	10,840	2,147	817	2,110	2,659	745	2,336
The Invisible Man Ch. 1-4	Novel	504	7,578	7,924	1,845	442	1,471	2,118	472	1,720
French Source										
Nuclear Testing	Public Info	613	13,127	13,563	3,918	1,412	1,808	4,261	1,344	2,253
French Revolution to 1945	Public Info	1530	34,038	33,187	11,217	3,119	4,279	11,008	3,025	4,632
The Immoralist	Novel	1,377	29,323	24,942	5,299	2,049	5,888	5,813	1,513	6,138
News article 1	News	126	1,757	1,751	549	122	284	558	115	324
News article 2	News	126	2,306	2,254	590	150	430	673	125	459
News article 3	News	85	1,891	1,756	501	183	332	534	122	332
News article 4	News	97	2,236	1,974	641	157	367	609	120	356

Table 1: Documents taken from the English (En) - French (Fr) section of the INTERSECT corpus.

French collection (Table 1). The frequencies for nouns (N), adjectives (A) and verbs (V) in this table were extracted automatically using the TreeTagger tool (Schmid, 1994).

Word alignments for the parallel documents were computed using Giza++ (Och and Ney, 2003) run in both directions. In order to improve the robustness of the word alignments the documents were concatenated into a single file, together with English-French parallel data from the Europarl corpus (Koehn, 2005). The word alignments for the relevant documents were then extracted from the symmetrised alignment file.

3.2 Consistency in Human Translation

The motivation for this analysis was to assess the extent to which a human translator maintained lexical consistency when translating a document. In other words, in those places where the author of a source document makes consistent lexical choices, do human translators do so as well? And if they do, should we aim for the same in SMT?

For each document, the English and French parallel texts were processed using TreeTagger (Schmid, 1994). Using the language in which the document was originally written (its *born language*) as the source language, word alignments were used to identify what each source word aligned to in the (human) translation.

Since I wanted to establish not just the *degree* of consistency, but *where* consistency was being maintained, and because I felt that the Part-of-Speech (POS) tags output by TreeTagger were too fine-grained for this purpose, these tags were mapped to a set of coarse-grained tags. The Universal POS tagset mapping file (Petrov et al., 2011) was used for English and a comparable file was constructed for French. In addition to this, I also sub-divided the coarse-grained verb class into three classes: light verbs (e.g. do, have, make), mid-range verbs (e.g. build, read, speak) and rare-verbs (e.g. revolutionise, obfuscate, perambulate). This was to test the hypothesis that light verbs will exhibit lower levels of consistency than other verbs. A *light verb* is defined a verb with little semantic content of its own that forms a predicate with its argument (usually a noun). For example the verb "do" in "do lunch" or "make" in "make a request". As no predefined lists of light, mid-range and rare verbs are available, these groups were approximated. An English verb's category is determined by its frequency in the British National Corpus (BNC) (Clear, 1993). A verb with a frequency count in the bottom 5% is deemed a rare verb, in the top 5% is deemed a light verb and anything in between, is deemed a mid-range verb. A manual inspection of the resulting category boundaries shows that these thresholds are reasonable. For French, verb frequencies were extracted from the French Treebank (Abeillé et al., 2000).

Herfindahl-Hirschman Index (HHI) (Itagaki et al., 2007) scores were calculated for each surface word (one score per surface word) in the *born language* document. The documents were treated separately, and no inter-document scores are calculated. These scores tell us how consistent the translation is into the target language. For words in the English documents I considered what words *and* lemmas were present in the French translation. Lemmas are included as French verb inflections may otherwise skew the results. For completeness, lemmas in the English translation of the French documents are also considered.

For each POS category, an average HHI score is calculated by taking the sum of the HHI scores per word and dividing it by the number of words (for that POS category). Only those words that are repeated (i.e. appear more than once in the source document with the same coarse POS category) are considered. (That is, a word that appeared once as a mid-range verb, once as a noun and once as something else, would not be included). A similar average is calculated for lemmas.

HHI scores are normally presented in the range of 0 to 10,000. However, for simplicity, the scores presented in this paper are normalised to between 0 to 1.

3.3 Consistency in Automated Translation

The aim of this analysis was to assess how the consistency in translations produced by an SMT system would compare to those by a human translator. The SMT system was an English-French phrase-based system trained and tuned using (Moses and) Europarl data. Its language model was constructed from the French side of the parallel training corpus. The system was used to translate the *born* English source documents (*Xerox Manual*, *On the Origin of Species*, *Dracula* and *The Invisible Man*). Word alignments and a file containing a list of Out of Vocabulary (OOV) words were also requested from the decoder. Note that *all* of the documents are considered to be "out of domain" with respect to the training data used to build the SMT system.

Using a similar process as described in Section 3.2, but omitting those words that are reported by the decoder as OOV, average HHI scores are calculated for each POS category. OOV words are omitted as these will be "carried through" by the decoder, appearing untranslated in the translation output. They therefore do not say anything about the consistency of the translation.

The other major difference is that HHI scores are calculated only at the word level, not at the lemma level as it is expected that the TreeTagger would perform poorly on SMT output and these errors could lead to misleading results. In all other respects, the process for analysing text is the same as described in Section 3.2.

4 Results

4.1 Consistency in Human Translation

The results are presented in Table 2. Higher (average) HHI scores represent greater consistency.

For both English and French source documents, nouns score highly, suggesting that in general human translators translate nouns rather consistently. However, nouns don't always receive the highest average score. For verbs, the trend is that consistency is irrelevant in translating light verbs, rare verbs tend to be translated with the highest consistency, and mid-range verbs are somewhere in between. This suggests that consistency in the translation of light verbs would be undesirable.

Looking at some of the texts in more detail it may be possible to infer certain qualities of text across different genres.

Novels: In all three texts, (*Dracula*, *The Invisible Man* and *The Immoralist*), nouns receive the highest average HHI score of all the POS categories. An analysis of some of the most frequent (and aligned) nouns in *Dracula* (Table 3) suggests that it is desirable to keep important nouns constant - those that identify characters and other entities central to the story. For example, the *Count* is an important character and is never referred to by any other name/title in the original text. (N.B. "count" is also a mid-range verb, but it is used only as a noun in *Dracula*). The translation to *(le) comte* in French is highly consistent. A similar observation is made for *horses* which are important in the story. Interestingly, the (same) coach *driver* is referred to as *(le) chauffer*, *(le) conducteur* and *(le) cocher* in French:

English: ...and the *driver* said in excellent German
French: Le *conducteur* me dit alors, en excellent allemand

English: Then the *driver* cracked his whip
French: Puis le *chauffeur* fit claquer son fouet

English: When the caleche stopped, the *driver* jumped down
French: La calèche arrêtée, le *cocher* sauta de son siège

This perhaps reflects a stylistic choice made by the translator to vary the terms used to refer to a character of lesser importance. It is worth noting that the English text also contains several instances of "coachman" to refer to the "driver" but the variation is much less compared with the French translation.

Verbs, on the other hand, receive lower (average) HHI scores indicating that this may be an area

Title	Noun	Adj	Verb			
			All	Light	Mid-Range	Rare
English Source						
Xerox ScanWorx Manual	**0.6995**	0.5900	0.5568	0.3256	0.5766	0.6485
Xerox ScanWorx Manual (Lemmas)	**0.7126**	0.7112	0.6612	0.4172	0.6902	0.7086
On the Origin of Species	**0.6109**	0.4390	0.4001	0.2339	0.4140	0.4592
On the Origin of Species (Lemmas)	**0.6417**	0.5722	0.5056	0.3355	0.5273	0.5098
Dracula	**0.6182**	0.4191	0.3631	0.2477	0.4175	0.5000
Dracula (Lemmas)	**0.6294**	0.4979	0.4113	0.2902	0.4711	0.5000
The Invisible Man	**0.6290**	0.5110	0.4159	0.3139	0.4797	0.4219
The Invisible Man (Lemmas)	**0.6275**	0.5743	0.4573	0.3723	0.5121	0.4219
French Source						
Nuclear Testing	0.7388	**0.8079**	0.5616	0.3312	0.5279	0.6228
Nuclear Testing (Lemmas)	0.7521	**0.8209**	0.5972	0.4198	0.5599	0.6584
French Revolution to 1945	0.6346	**0.6587**	0.5054	0.3041	0.4404	0.5521
French Revolution to 1945 (Lemmas)	0.6509	**0.6632**	0.5266	0.3950	0.4710	0.5655
The Immoralist	**0.6807**	0.5732	0.4868	0.3106	0.4524	0.5046
The Immoralist (Lemmas)	**0.7007**	0.5856	0.5142	0.3821	0.4977	0.5236
News article 1	**0.7278**	0.6400	0.5424	0.4336	0.5608	0.5734
News article 1 (Lemmas)	**0.7542**	0.6400	0.5616	0.4943	0.5608	0.5911
News article 2	0.6745	**0.7140**	0.5345	0.3660	0.5395	0.6751
News article 2 (Lemmas)	0.6836	0.7140	0.5717	0.4083	0.5395	**0.7778**
News article 3	0.6991	**0.7986**	0.5024	0.3016	0.5794	0.5988
News article 3 (Lemmas)	0.7121	**0.7986**	0.5869	0.4801	0.6508	0.6204
News article 4	**0.6734**	0.6556	0.5073	0.2408	0.6667	0.6295
News article 4 (Lemmas)	0.6984	0.6333	0.6118	0.3790	0.6667	**0.7545**

Table 2: Human Translation: Average HHI scores for words in the source and their aligned words (and lemmas) in the translations. Scores are provided in the range of 0 to 1 and the highest score for each document is highlighted in bold text. The scores for rare verbs in Dracula and The Invisible Man are the same for words and lemmas. These documents contain very few repeated rare verbs (far fewer than the other English documents) and those that are repeated are very specific and diverse such that no difference is seen between the two distributions.

Noun (word)	HHI score	Count
Count	0.9412	33
driver	0.2985	28
horses	0.9050	20
room	0.4000	20
time	0.1150	20
door	0.5986	17
place	0.6797	16
night	0.4667	15

Table 3: Dracula - most frequent noun words

in which some artistic license may be used.

These findings suggest that when aiming to encourage consistency in the translation of novels, the focus should be on nouns. As for adjectives, less frequent in novels than verbs and nouns (Table 1), further analysis may show whether consistency varies depending on function (e.g. modifier, predicate adjective) or frequency as well. The translation of pronouns also requires investigation.

Natural Science: The natural science text *On the Origin of Species* exhibits a similar pattern of translational consistency to novels. This is perhaps not surprising as 19th century British natural science texts would have had the same middle-class audience as the novels of the same era. The translation of modern scientific texts may or may not follow this pattern.

Instruction Manuals: In the *Xerox Manual* nouns receive the highest average HHI score at the word level. When considering what lemmas the source words align to in the translation, nouns again score the highest, closely followed by adjectives and rare verbs. This overall pattern makes sense as in an instruction manual it is important to identify both the actions and entities involved at each step. Adjectives will help the user correctly identify the intended entities. The word-level HHI scores for the most frequently used (and aligned) rare verbs are given in Table 4.

The verb *process* has several translations in French: *traitement* ("treatment"/"processing"), *traiter* ("process") and *exécuter* ("execute"). (Note that *traitement* is in fact a noun, reflecting a change in the structure of the sentence.) The

Rare Verb (word)	HHI score	Count
process	0.5729	109
previewing	0.5868	33
previewed	0.6399	19
verifying	0.5556	18
formatted	0.3244	15
scans	1.0000	13
formatting	0.4380	11
dithering	0.4380	11

Table 4: Xerox Manual - most frequent rare verb words

Adjective (word)	HHI score	Count
nationale (*national*)	0.8233	75
européenne (*European*)	0.8232	64
économique (*economic*)	0.8575	40
constitutionnel (*constitutional*)	0.9474	37
française (*French*)	0.4288	37
constitutionnelle (*constitutional*)	1.0000	31
français (*French*)	0.7899	26
autres (*other*)	0.8496	25

Table 5: French Revolution to 1945 - most frequent adjective words

resulting translations into French are all clear, so this may simply be a reflection of a difference in terminology between English and French, at least as used by Xerox. For example:

English: *Process* the page and save the output as an image.
French: *Traitement* de la page et sauvegarde de la sortie comme image.

English: Page Settings enable you to describe the pages that the system is about to *process*.
French: Les Instructions de page vous permettent de décrire les pages que le système va *traiter*.

English: Load Verification Data, Loads a named verification data file to *process* a job.
French: Charger données de vérification, Charge un fichier nommé de données de vérification pour *exécuter* une tâche.

What is also interesting is that in the English text, the word *process* is used as both a noun and a rare verb. However, it is translated more consistently when used as a verb (HHI: 0.5729) compared with its use as a noun (HHI: 0.2576).

In this genre, accuracy and readability are important and it is acceptable to produce a "repetitive" or "boring" text. It may, therefore, be appropriate to encourage translational consistency of nouns, rare verbs and adjectives in instructions. Unlike with novels, it would make sense that *all* entities in an instruction manual are of importance.

Public Information: In the *French Revolution to 1945* and *Nuclear Testing* documents, adjectives score highest, followed by nouns. Word-level HHI scores for the most frequent (and aligned) adjectives in the *French Revolution to 1945* document are presented in Table 5.

Using a manual inspection of those nouns that appear next to (i.e. directly after) the adjective in French, the possibility that these nouns were *semantically light* was explored. Focussing on the English translation, WordNet (Miller, 1995) was used to ascertain the distance of the noun from the root of the relevant hierarchy. The assumption is the semantically light nouns appear closer to the root than other nouns. For all 82,115 noun synsets in WordNet, the average minimum and maximum depths to the root are 7.25 and 7.70 respectively.

Taking the adjective *economic* (*économique* in French) in the *French Revolution to 1945* document as an example, the nouns it is paired with (e.g. expansion, cooperation, development, action, council, etc.) typically have depths below the average and therefore could be considered semantically light. The adjectives used in the text include *constitutionnel / constitutionnelle* ("constitutional"), *économique* ("economic") and *nationale* ("national"). These words are rather specific (or "semantically heavy"), so there may be few alternative valid translations to choose from. This is supported by Melamed's (1997) notion of semantic entropy, in which more specific words receive lower entropy scores, reflecting greater consistency in translation. For texts of this genre, it may be appropriate to encourage the consistent translation of adjectives and nouns, allowing for more freedom in the translation of verbs.

News Articles: The pattern for news articles is a little less predictable, although a similar pattern (to other document types) can be seen for light, mid-range and rare verbs. This may be due to the short length of the texts (circa 2,000 words) which may not be sufficient to establish a stable pattern. Or it may be that there are different writing styles within the news genre dependent on the type or subject of the "story".

4.2 Consistency in Automated Translation

The results of a similar analysis of translational consistency in phrase-based SMT are presented in Table 6. Overall, consistency is much higher than in translations produced by human translators. But what does this mean? Is the problem of consistency in SMT non-existent? In short, no; there are

POS Category	Xerox Manual		Origin of Species		Dracula		The Invisible Man	
	Automated	Human	Automated	Human	Automated	Human	Automated	Human
Noun	0.8502	0.6995	0.8481	0.6109	0.8318	0.6182	0.8308	0.6290
Adj	0.6871	0.5900	0.6333	0.4390	0.6543	0.4191	0.6966	0.5110
Verb (all)	0.7131	0.5568	0.6023	0.4001	0.5764	0.3631	0.5829	0.4159
Light Verb	0.4919	0.3256	0.4538	0.2339	0.4310	0.2477	0.4873	0.3139
Mid-Range Verb	0.7160	0.5766	0.5927	0.4140	0.6301	0.4175	0.6271	0.4797
Rare Verb	0.8955	0.6485	0.8195	0.4592	0.8571	0.5000	0.8750	0.4218

Table 6: Automated Translation: Average HHI scores taken for words in automated translations as compared with the scores from human translations. Scores are provided in the range of 0 to 1

still areas in which consistency is a real problem, but one needs to look more closely at the data to find the problems.

Any consistency in the output of an SMT system will be accidental, and not by design. It is a reflection of the data that the system was trained with and represents the "best" choice for translating a word or phrase, as determined by scores from the phrase table and language model. Carpuat and Simard (2012) suggest that consistency in the source side local context may be sufficient to constrain the phrase table and language model to produce consist translations. It is also important to note that the outcome is very much dependent on the system used to perform the translation. Carpuat and Simard (2012) suggest that weaker SMT systems (i.e. those that report lower BLEU scores) may be more consistent than their stronger counterparts due to fewer translation options.

There are several possibilities. A word in the source language may be translated:

- Completely consistently (HHI = 1);
- Very inconsistently (HHI $\sim$ 0);
- or anywhere in between

Additionally, a translation that is deemed to be completely consistent may be either correct or incorrect. With humans, we assume the translation output to be of a high standard but we cannot assume the same of an SMT system.

Examples of completely consistent translations are *horses* as "chevaux", *man* as "homme" and *nails* as "clous". All are taken from *Dracula*. While *horses* and *man* are translated correctly, "clous" is an incorrect translation of *nails* which the context of the novel refer to Dracula's fingernails. "ongles" would have been the correct translation. The word "clous" is typically used in the sense of nails used in construction. This is an example of a translation that could result either from lack of sufficient local context (for disambiguation) or because "ongles" is not present in the data the SMT system was trained on.

Examples of inconsistent translations are for the body parts *arm* and *hand* in the text of *Dracula*. *arm* is translated either correctly as "bras" (arm, body part) or incorrectly as "armer" (the verb "to arm"). *hand* is translated correctly as "main" ("hand") and incorrectly as côté ("side") and "part" ("portion"). In both cases, the correct translation was available to the system and a more accurate translation could have been obtained had the correct translation been identified and its consistency encouraged.

Ambiguous words in particular can cause trouble for SMT systems. There are many words that can function as both a verb and a noun, e.g. *process* and *count*. Local context might not always be sufficient to provide the correct disambiguation, resulting in opportunities for incorrect translations.

An example of where an ambiguous word results in problems is in the translation of *count* (i.e. Count Dracula) as: omitted (4), "compter" (21), "compatage" (2), "comte" (1) and "dépouillement" (5). The only acceptable translation from this set is "comte". As for the reaming options: "compte" and "comptage" are both verbs meaning "to count" and "dépouillement" is a noun meaning "starkness", "austerity" or "analysis" (of data).

5 Conclusion

The analysis of human translation presented in this paper is a first attempt to understand where and when it might be appropriate to encourage consistency in an SMT system. I consider genre as the *where* and parts-of-speech as the *when*, but other interpretations are also possible. On the whole, it seems reasonable to encourage the consistent translation of nouns, across all genres. In addition, encouraging consistency in the translation of rare verbs and adjectives for technical documents and of adjectives for public information documents may also prove beneficial.

With respect to verbs, variation in verb consistency has been shown to correlate with frequency (as a proxy to identify light and rare verbs). Given the low consistency with which humans translate light verbs, encouraging their consistency in automated translation would be undesirable.

Automated translation may look very consistent on the surface, but it is necessary to look beyond this to see the errors. While humans may make inconsistent translations, we trust that these inconsistencies will not confuse or mislead the reader. SMT systems on the other hand generate their translations based on statistics that say what the "best choice" might be, both at the word/phrase level (through the phrase table) and overall (through the language model). Furthermore, they do nothing to guarantee consistency - this occurs by chance, whether desirable or not. As a result, inconsistencies may arise that make the translations difficult to read. These inconsistencies are not predictable and could occur in any SMT system.

6 Future Work

The findings presented in this paper are suggestive but only a small number of texts have been included for each genre. The analysis could be extended to include a larger set of documents and different language pairs (the only requirement is for a POS tagger for the source language). Multiple translations of the same document could also be considered to identify whether similar patterns can be observed for different translators.

There are a number of possible ways in which to use this information to inform the design of a SMT system. I have shown that SMT systems are capable of highly consistent translations but this consistency cannot be guaranteed and there is the possibility that the translations will be consistent and incorrect. Also, Carpuat and Simard (2012) have shown that inconsistent translations in SMT often indicate translation errors. A system which encourages translations which are both consistent and correct (or at least acceptable) for words that belong to a predefined set (e.g. by POS tag) is desirable. This "encouragement" could be achieved using rewards delivered via feature functions or within n-best list re-ranking – hypotheses which make re-use of the same translation(s) for repetitions of the same source word would be ranked higher than those that introduced inconsistencies. Revisiting the cache-based models of (2010a; 2010b) and Gong et al. (2011) could provide a possible starting point.

The initial focus could be on nouns, which are translated by human translators with high consistency for all genres. Many nouns are used either to specify entities that are only mentioned once in a text (essentially setting the scene for more prominent entities), or as "predicate nominals" on those more prominent entities (e.g. in "...is a horrific *story*"). However, other nouns occur within the Noun Phrases (NPs) that make up part of a *coreference chain*, of subsequent reference to prominent entities.

As an extension to this work I will aim to investigate the consistency of translation of those nouns that belong to coreference chains and ultimately, to build a system that makes use of the resulting information. Work has already started to construct a parallel corpus in which coreference chains are annotated so that the translation of coreference (both NPs and pronouns) may be studied in more depth.

Another question worth considering is whether it would be desirable to replicate aspects of low consistency in human translation by encouraging inconsistent (but still acceptable) translations of certain words or word categories. My instinct is that this could lead to translations that better approximate those produced by humans.

7 Acknowledgements

The research leading to these results has received funding from the European Union Seventh Framework Programme (FP7/2007-2013) under grant agreement 287658 (EU BRIDGE). Thanks to Professor Bonnie Webber for her guidance and numerous helpful suggestions and to the three anonymous reviewers for their feedback.

References

Anne Abeillé, Lionel Clément, and Alexandra Kinyon. 2000. Building a treebank for french. In *In Proceedings of the LREC 2000*.

Marine Carpuat and Michel Simard. 2012. The trouble with smt consistency. In *Proceedings of the Seventh Workshop on Statistical Machine Translation*, WMT

'12, pages 442–449, Stroudsburg, PA, USA. Association for Computational Linguistics.

Marine Carpuat. 2009. One translation per discourse. In *Proceedings of the Workshop on Semantic Evaluations: Recent Achievements and Future Directions*, DEW '09, pages 19–27, Stroudsburg, PA, USA. Association for Computational Linguistics.

Jeremy H. Clear. 1993. The digital word. chapter The British national corpus, pages 163–187. MIT Press, Cambridge, MA, USA.

William A. Gale, Kenneth W. Church, and David Yarowsky. 1992. One sense per discourse. In *Proceedings of the workshop on Speech and Natural Language*, HLT '91, pages 233–237, Stroudsburg, PA, USA. Association for Computational Linguistics.

Zhengxian Gong, Min Zhang, and Guodong Zhou. 2011. Cache-based document-level statistical machine translation. In *Proceedings of the Conference on Empirical Methods in Natural Language Processing*, EMNLP '11, pages 909–919, Stroudsburg, PA, USA. Association for Computational Linguistics.

Michael A.K. Halliday and Ruqaiya Hasan. 1976. *Cohesion in English*. Longman, London.

Yifan He, Yanjun Ma, Andy Way, and Josef van Genabith. 2011. Rich linguistic features for translation memory-inspired consistent translatio. In *Proceedings of Machine Translation Summit XIII*, pages 456–463.

Masaki Itagaki, Takako Aikawa, and Xiaodon He. 2007. Automatic validation of terminology consistency with statistical method. In *Proceedings of Machine Translation Summit XI*, pages 269–274. European Associaton for Machine Translation.

Philipp Koehn. 2005. Europarl: A Parallel Corpus for Statistical Machine Translation. In *Conference Proceedings: the tenth Machine Translation Summit*, pages 79–86. AAMT, AAMT.

Kazem Lotfipour-Saedi. 1997. Lexical cohesion and translation equivalence. *Meta: Journal des Traducteurs / Meta: Translators' Journal*, 42(1):185–192.

Yanjun Ma, Yifan He, Andy Way, and Josef van Genabith. 2011. Consistent translation using discriminative learning: a translation memory-inspired approach. In *Proceedings of the 49th Annual Meeting of the Association for Computational Linguistics: Human Language Technologies - Volume 1*, HLT '11, pages 1239–1248, Stroudsburg, PA, USA. Association for Computational Linguistics.

I. Dan Melamed. 1997. Measuring semantic entropy. In *Proceedings of the SIGLEX Workshop on Tagging Text with Lexical Semantics*, pages 41–46.

George A. Miller. 1995. Wordnet: A lexical database for english. *Commun. ACM*, 38(11):39–41, November.

Jane Morris and Graeme Hirst. 1991. Lexical cohesion computed by thesaural relations as an indicator of the structure of text. *Comput. Linguist.*, 17(1):21–48, March.

Franz Josef Och and Hermann Ney. 2003. A systematic comparison of various statistical alignment models. *Computational Linguistics*, 29:19–51, March.

Slav Petrov, Dipanjan Das, and Ryan McDonald. 2011. A universal part-of-speech tagset. In *IN ARXIV:1104.2086*.

Raphael Salkie. 2010. The intersect translation corpus. Available on the web: http://arts.brighton.ac.uk/staff/raf-salkie/portfolio-of-major-works/intersect.

Helmut Schmid. 1994. Probabilistic part-of-speech tagging using decision trees. In *Proceedings of International Conference on New Methods in Language Processing*.

Jörg Tiedemann. 2010a. Context adaptation in statistical machine translation using models with exponentially decaying cache. In *Proceedings of the 2010 Workshop on Domain Adaptation for Natural Language Processing*, DANLP 2010, pages 8–15, Stroudsburg, PA, USA. Association for Computational Linguistics.

Jörg Tiedemann. 2010b. To cache or not to cache? experiments with adaptive models in statistical machine translation. In *Proceedings of the Joint Fifth Workshop on Statistical Machine Translation and Metrics MATR*, pages 189–194, Uppsala, Sweden, July. Association for Computational Linguistics.

Ferhan Ture, Douglas W. Oard, and Philip Resnik. 2012. Encouraging consistent translation choices. In *Proceedings of the 2012 Conference of the North American Chapter of the Association for Computational Linguistics: Human Language Technologies*, NAACL HLT '12, pages 417–426, Stroudsburg, PA, USA. Association for Computational Linguistics.

Tong Xiao, Jingbo Zhu, and Shujie Yao. 2011. Document-level consistency verification in machine translation. In *Proceedings of MT summit XIII*, pages 131–138.

Implicitation of Discourse Connectives in (Machine) Translation

Thomas Meyer
Idiap Research Institute and EPFL
Martigny and Lausanne, Switzerland
thomas.meyer@idiap.ch

Bonnie Webber
University of Edinburgh
Edinburgh, UK
bonnie@inf.ed.ac.uk

Abstract

Explicit discourse connectives in a source language text are not always translated to comparable words or phrases in the target language. The paper provides a corpus analysis and a method for semi-automatic detection of such cases. Results show that discourse connectives are not translated into comparable forms (or even any form at all), in up to 18% of human reference translations from English to French or German. In machine translation, this happens much less frequently (up to 8% only). Work in progress aims to capture this natural implicitation of discourse connectives in current statistical machine translation models.

1 Introduction

Discourse connectives (DCs), a class of frequent cohesive markers, such as *although, however, for example, in addition, since, while, yet*, etc., are especially prone to 'translationese', i.e. the use of constructions in the target language (TL) that differ in frequency or position from how they would be found in texts born in the language. That is, 'translationese' makes DCs prone to being translated in ways that can differ markedly from their use in the source language. (Blum-Kulka, 1986; Cartoni et al., 2011; Ilisei et al., 2010; Halverson, 2004; Hansen-Schirra et al., 2007; Zufferey et al., 2012). For cohesive markers and DCs, Koppel and Ordan (2011) and Cartoni et al. (2011) have shown that they may be more explicit (increased use) or less explicit (decreased use) in translationese. The paper focuses on the latter case, but the same detection method can be applied in reverse, in order to find increased use (explicitation) as well.

In English about 100 types of explicit DCs have been annotated in the Penn Discourse TreeBank, or PDTB (Prasad et al., 2008) (We say more about this in Section 3.1). The actual set of markers or connectives is however rather open-ended (Prasad et al., 2010). DCs signal discourse relations that connect two spans of text and can be ambiguous with respect to the discourse relation they convey. Moreover, the same DC can simultaneously convey more than one discourse relation. For example, *while* can convey contrast or temporality, or both at the same time. On the other hand, discourse relations can also be conveyed implicitly, without an explicit DC.

Human translators can chose to not translate a SL DC with a TL DC, where the latter would be redundant or where the SL discourse relation would more naturally be conveyed in the TL by other means (cf. Section 2). We will use the term 'zero-translation' or 'implicitation' for a valid translation that conveys the same sense as a lexically explicit SL connective, but not with the same form. As we will show, current SMT models either learn the explicit lexicalization of a SL connective to a TL connective, or treat the former as a random variation, realizing it or not. Learning other valid ways of conveying the same discourse relation might not only result in more fluent TL text, but also help raise its BLEU score by more closely resembling its more implicit human reference text.

The paper presents work in progress on a corpus study where zero-translations of DCs have been semi-automatically detected in human reference and machine translations from English (EN) to French (FR) and German (DE) (Section 3). Two types of discourse relations that are very frequently omitted in FR and DE translations are studied in detail and we outline features on how these omissions could be modeled into current SMT systems (Section 4).

2 Implicitation of connectives in translation

Figure 1 is an extract from a news article in the newstest2010 data set (see Section 3.2). It contains two EN connectives — *as* and *otherwise* — that were annotated in the PDTB[1]. Using the set of discourse relations of the PDTB, *as* can be said to signal the discourse relation CAUSE (subtype Reason), and *otherwise* the discourse relation ALTERNATIVE. This is discussed further in Section 3.1.

EN: The man with the striking bald head was still needing a chauffeur, **1. as** the town was still unknown to him. **2. Otherwise** he could have driven himself — **3. after all**, no alcohol was involved and the 55-year-old was not drunk.

FR-REF: L'homme, dont le crâne chauve attirait l'attention, se laissa conduire **1. __0__** dans la ville qui lui était encore étrangère. **2. Autrement** notre quinquagénaire aurait pu prendre lui-même le volant — **3. __0__** il n'avait pas bu d'alcool et il n'était pas non plus ivre de bonheur.

DE-REF: Der Mann mit der markanten Glatze liess sich **1. wegen/Prep** der ihm noch fremden Stadt chauffieren. **2. Ansonsten** hätte er auch selbst fahren können — Alkohol war **3. schliesslich/Adv** nicht im Spiel, und besoffen vor Glück war der 55-jährige genauso wenig.

Figure 1: Examples of EN source connectives translated as zero or by other means in human reference translations.

The human reference translations do not translate the first connective *as* explicitly. In FR there is no direct equivalent, and the reason why the man needed a driver is given with a relative clause: *...dans la ville qui...* (lit.: in the town that was still foreign to him). In DE *as* is realized by means of a preposition, *wegen* (lit.: because of). The second EN connective *otherwise*, maintains its form in translation to the target connective *autrement* in FR and *ansonsten* in DE.

On the other hand, baseline SMT systems for EN/FR and EN/DE (Section 3.2) both translated the two connectives *as* and *otherwise* explicitly by the usual target connectives, in FR: *comme, sinon* and in DE *wie, sonst*.

3 Semi-automatic detection of zero-translations

3.1 Method

The semi-automatic method that identifies zero- or non-connective translations in human references and machine translation output is based on a list of 48 EN DCs with a frequency above 20 in the Penn Discourse TreeBank Version 2.0 (Prasad et al., 2008). In order to identify which discourse relations are most frequently translated as zero, we have assigned each of the EN DCs the level-2 discourse relation that it is most frequently associated with in the PDTB corpus. The total list of EN connectives is given in Table 1.

For every source connective, we queried its most frequent target connective translations from the online dictionary Linguee[2] and added them to dictionaries of possible FR and DE equivalents.

With these dictionaries and Giza++ word alignment (Och and Ney, 2003), the SL connectives can be located and the sentences of its translation (reference and/or automatic) can be scanned for an aligned occurrence of the TL dictionary entries. If more than one DC appears in the source sentence and/or a DC is not aligned with a connective or connective-equivalent found in the dictionaries, the word position (word index) of the SL connective is compared to the word indexes of the translation in order to detect whether a TL connective (or connective-equivalent from the dictionaries) appears in a 5-word window to its left and right.[3]. This also helps filtering out cases of non-connective uses of e.g. *separately* or *once* as adverbs. Finally, if no aligned entry is present and the alignment information remains empty, the method counts a zero-translation and collects statistics on these occurrences.

After a first run where we only allowed for actual connectives as translation dictionary entries, we manually looked through 400 cases for each, FR and DE reference translations, that were output

[1]The excerpt contains a third possible connective *after all* that was not annotated in the PDTB, and our data as a whole contains other possible connectives not yet annotated there, including *given that* and *at the same time*. We did not analyse such possible connectives in the work described here.

[2]`http://www.linguee.com`

[3]The method extends on the ACT metric (Hajlaoui and Popescu-Belis, 2013) that measures MT quality in terms of connectives in order to detect more types of DCs and their equivalents.

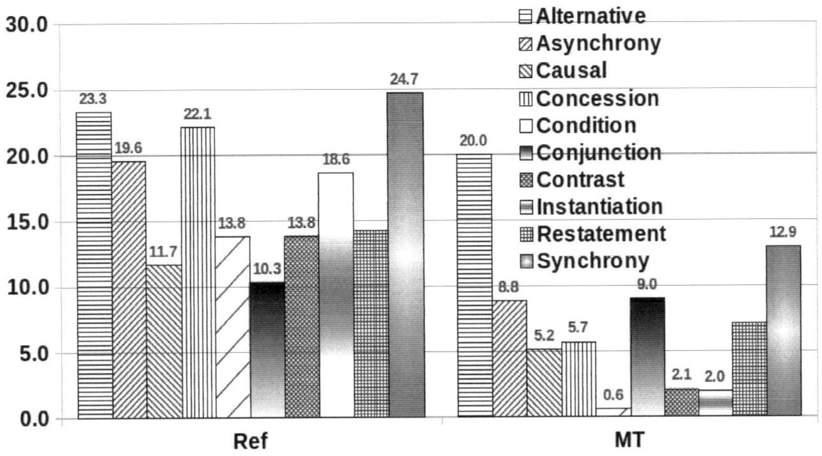

Figure 2: Percentage of zero-translations in newstest2010+2012 for EN/FR per discourse relation and translation type: human reference (Ref) or MT output (MT).

as zero-translations (in the newtest2012 data, see Section 3.2). We found up to 100 additional cases that actually were not implicitations, but conveyed the SL connective's meaning by means of a paraphrase, e.g. EN: *if* – FR: *dans le cas où* (lit.: in case where) – DE: *im Falle von* (lit.: in case of). For example, the EN connective *otherwise* ended up with the dictionary entries in Figure 3.

EN: **otherwise** ALTERNATIVE :
FR: autrement|sinon|car|dans un autre cas|d'une autre manière
DE: ansonsten|andernfalls|anderenfalls |anderweitig|widrigenfalls|andrerseits| andererseits|anders|sonst

Figure 3: Dictionary entries of FR and DE connectives and equivalents for the EN connective *otherwise*.

3.2 Data

For the experiments described here, we concatenated two data sets, the newstest2010 and newstest2012 parallel texts as publicly available by the Workshop on Machine Translation[4]. The texts consist of complete articles from various daily news papers that have been translated from EN to FR, DE and other languages by translation agencies.

In total, there are 5,492 sentences and 117,799 words in the SL texts, of which 2,906 are tokens of the 48 EN connectives. See Table 1 for the connectives and their majority class, which aggregate to the detailed statistics given in Table 2.

Rel.	TC	Rel.	TC
Alternative	30	Conjunction	329
Asynchrony	588	Contrast	614
Cause	308	Instantiation	43
Concession	140	Restatement	14
Condition	159	Synchrony	681

Table 2: Total counts (TC) of English discourse connectives (2,906 tokens) from the newstest2010+2012 corpora, whose majority sense conveys one of the 10 PDTB level-2 discourse relations (Rel.) listed here.

To produce machine translations of the same data sets we built EN/FR and EN/DE baseline phrase-based SMT systems, by using the Moses decoder (Koehn et al., 2007), with the Europarl corpus v7 (Koehn, 2005) as training and newtest2011 as tuning data. The 3-gram language model was built with IRSTLM (Federico et al., 2008) over Europarl and the rest of WMT's news data for FR and DE.

3.3 Results

In order to group the individual counts of zero-translations per DC according to the discourse relation they signal, we calculated the relative frequency of zero-translations per relation as percentages, see Figures 2 for EN/FR, and 4 for EN/DE.

[4]http://www.statmt.org/wmt12/

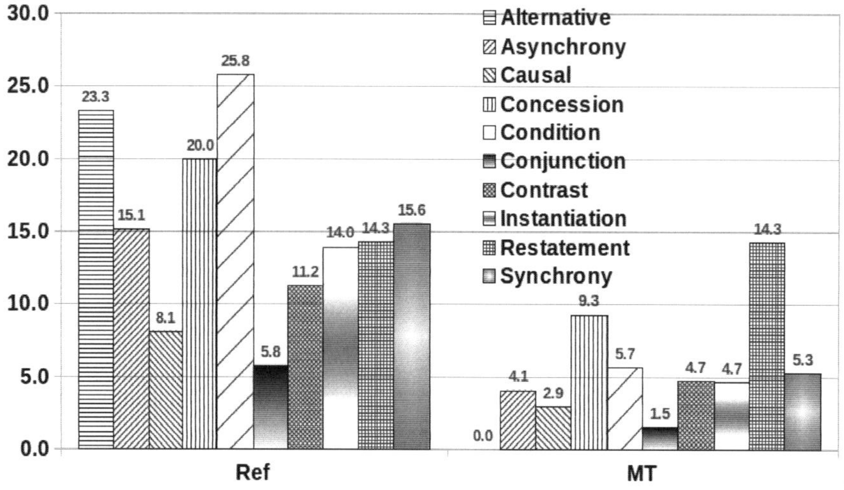

Figure 4: Percentage of zero-translations in newstest2010+2012 for EN/DE per discourse relation and translation type: human reference (Ref) or MT output (MT).

The total percentage of zero-translations in the references and the baseline MT output is given in Table 3.

A first observation is that an MT system seems to produce zero-translations for DCs significantly less often than human translators do. Human FR translations seem to have a higher tendency toward omitting connectives than the ones in DE. Figures 2 and 4 also show that the discourse relations that are most often rendered as zero are dependent on the TL. In the FR reference translations, SYNCHRONY, ALTERNATIVE and CONCESSION account for most implicitations, while in the DE reference translations, CONDITION, ALTERNATIVE and CONCESSION are most often left implicit.

Translation	Type	C	%
EN/FR	Ref	508	17.5
	MT	217	7.5
EN/DE	Ref	392	13.5
	MT	129	4.4

Table 3: Counts (C) and relative frequency (%) of zero-translations for EN/FR and EN/DE in human references (Ref) and MT output (MT) over newstest2010+2012.

The results are to some extent counterintuitive as one would expect that semantically dense discourse relations like CONCESSION would need to be explicit in translation in order to convey the same meaning. Section 4 presents some non-connective means available in the two TLs, by which the discourse relations are still established.

We furthermore looked at the largest implicitation differences per discourse relation in the human reference translations and the MT output. For EN/FR for example, 13.8% of all CONDITION relations are implicitated in the references, by making use of paraphrases such as *dans le moment où* (lit.: in the moment where) or *dans votre cas* (lit.: in your case) in place of the EN connective *if*. The MT system translates *if* in 99.4% of all cases to the explicit FR connective *si*. Similarly, for INSTANTIATION relations and the EN connective *for instance* in the references, the translators made constrained use of verbal paraphrases such as *on y trouve* (lit.: among which we find). MT on the other hand outputs the explicit FR connective *par exemple* in all cases of *for instance*.

For EN/DE, there is the extreme case, where ALTERNATIVE relations are, in human reference translations, quite often implicitated (in 23.3% of all cases), whereas the MT system translates all the instances explicitly to DE connectives: *wenn* (unless), *sonst* (otherwise) and *statt, stattdessen, anstatt* (instead). The translators however make use of constructions with a sentence-initial verb in conditional mood (cf. Section 4.2) for *otherwise* and *unless*, but not for *instead*, which is, as with MT, always explicitly translated by humans, most often to the DE connective *statt*. The very opposite takes place for the RESTATEMENT relation and the EN connective *in fact*. Here, MT leaves implicit just as many instances as human translators do, i.e. 14.3% of all cases. Translators use paraphrases such as *in Wahrheit* (lit.: in truth) or *übrigens* (lit.: by the way), while the translation model tends to use *im Gegenteil* (lit.: opposite), which is not a literal translation of *in fact* (usually *in der Tat* or *tatsächlich* in DE), but reflects the contrastive function this marker frequently had in the Europarl training data of the baseline MT system.

4 Case studies

4.1 Temporal connectives from EN to FR

The most frequent implicitated discourse relation for EN/FR translation is SYNCHRONY, i.e. connectives conveying that their arguments describe events that take place at the same time. However, since the situations in which SYNCHRONY relations are implicitated are similar to those in which CONTRAST relations are implicitated, we discuss the two together.

We exemplify here cases where EN DCs that signal SYNCHRONY and/or CONTRAST are translated to FR with a '*en*/Preposition + Verb in Gerund' construction without a TL connective. The EN source instances giving rise to such implicitations in FR are usually of the form 'DC + Verb in Present Continuous' or 'DC + Verb in Simple Past', see sentences 1 and 2 in Figure 5.

Out of 13 cases of implicitations for *while* in the data, 8 (61.5%) have been translated to the mentioned construction in FR, as illustrated in the first example in Figure 5, with a reference and machine translation from newstest2010. The DC *while* here ambiguously signals SYNCHRONY and/or CONTRAST, but there is a second temporal marker (*at the same time*, a connective-equivalent not yet considered in this paper or in the PDTB), that disambiguates *while* to its CONTRAST sense only or to the composite sense SYNCHRONY/CONTRAST. The latter is conveyed in FR by *en méprisant*, with CONTRAST being reinforced by *tout* (lit.: all).

In Example 2, from newstest2012, the sentence-initial connective *when*, again signaling SYNCHRONY, is translated to the very same construction of '*en*/Preposition + Verb in Gerund' in the FR reference.

In the baseline MT output for Example 1, neither of the two EN DCs is deleted, *while* is literally translated to *alors que* and *at the same time* to *dans le même temps*. While the MT output is not totally wrong, it sounds disfluent, as *dans le même temps* after *alors que* is neither necessary nor appropriate.

In the baseline MT output for Example 2, the direct lexical equivalent for *when* – *lorsque* is generated, which is correct, although the translation has other mistakes such as the wrong verb *semblait* and the untranslated *weather-beaten*.

To model such cases for SMT one could use POS tags to detect the 'DC + Present Continuous/Simple Past' in EN and apply a rule to translate it to 'Preposition + Gerund' in FR. Furthermore, when two DCs follow each other in EN, and both can signal the *same* discourse relations, a word-deletion feature (as it is available in the Moses decoder via sparse features), could be used to trigger the deletion of one of the EN connectives, so that only one is translated to the TL. We

1. EN: In her view, the filmmaker "is asking a favour from the court, **while** at the same time **showing** disregard for its authority".
FR-REF: Pour elle, le cinéaste "demande une faveur à la cour, tout **en/Prep méprisant/V/Ger** son autorité".
FR-MT*: Dans son avis, le réalisateur de "demande une faveur de la cour, **alors que** dans le même temps une marque de mépris pour son autorité".

2. EN: **When** Meder **looked** through the weather-beaten windows of the red, white and yellow Art Nouveau building, she could see weeds growing up through the tiles.
FR-REF: **En/Prep jetant/V/Ger** un coup d'œil par la fenêtre de l'immeuble-art nouveau en rouge-blanc-jaune, elle a observé l'épanouissement des mauvaises herbes entre les carreaux.
FR-MT*: **Lorsque** Meder semblait weather-beaten à travers les fenêtres du rouge, jaune et blanc de l'art nouveau bâtiment, elle pourrait voir les mauvaises herbes qui grandissent par les tuiles.

Figure 5: Translation examples for the EN temporal connectives *while* and *when*, rendered in the FR reference as a 'preposition + Verb in Gerund' construction. MT generates the direct lexical equivalents *alors que* and *lorsque*.

will examine in future work whether there are systematic patterns in the translation of such 'double' connectives in SL and TL. Another possibility would be to treat cases like *while at the same time* as a multi-word phrase that is then translated to the corresponding prepositional construction in FR.

4.2 Conditional connectives from EN to DE

Out of the 41 cases involving a CONDITION relation (10.5% of all DE implicitations), 40 or 97.6% were due to the EN connective *if* not being translated to its DE equivalents *wenn*, *falls*, *ob*. Instead, in 21 cases (52.5%), the human reference translations made use of a verbal construction which obviates the need for a connective in DE when the verb in the *if*-clause is moved to sentence-initial position and its mood is made conditional, as in Figure 6, a reference translation from newstest2012, with the DE verb *wäre* (lit.: were) (VMFIN=modal finite verb, Konj=conditional). This construction is also available in EN (*Were you here, I would...*), but seems to be much more formal and less frequent than in DE where it is ordinarily used across registers. In the baseline MT output for this sentence, *if* was translated explicitly to the DE connective *wenn*, which is in principle correct, but the syntax of the translation is wrong, mainly due to the position of the verb *tun*, which should be at the end of the sentence.

The remaining 19 cases of EN *if* were either translated to DE prepositions (e.g. *bei, wo*, lit.: at, where) or the CONDITION relation is not expressed at all and verbs in indicative mood make the use of a conditional DE connective superfluous.

Of the 21 tokens of *if* whose reference translations used a verbal construction in DE, 14 (66.7%) were tokens of *if* whose argument clause explicitly referred to the preceding context – e.g., *if they were*, *if so*, *if this is true* etc. These occurrences could therefore be identified in EN and could be modeled for SMT as re-ordering rules on the verbal phrase in the DE syntax tree after constituent parsing in syntax-based translation models.

EN: **If** not for computer science, they would be doing amazing things in other fields.

DE-REF: __0__ **Wäre/VMFIN/Konj** es nicht die Computerbranche gewesen, würden sie in anderen Bereichen fantastische Dinge schaffen.

DE-MT*: **Wenn** nicht für die Informatik, würden sie tun, erstaunlich, Dinge auf anderen Gebieten.

Figure 6: Translation example for the EN connective *if*, rendered in the DE reference as a construction with a sentence-initial verb in conditional mood. MT generates the direct lexical equivalent *wenn*.

5 Conclusion

This study showed that human translators do not translate explicit EN discourse connectives as FR or DE discourse connectives in up to 18% of all cases. In MT output this happens about 3 times less often. We thus plan to examine how to produce higher-scoring translations without a target language connective but with some other syntactic pattern that conveys the same source language discourse relation. Depending on the features identified, movements of syntactical constituents or reordering of POS tags at the phrase and/or sub-tree level will be implemented for hierarchical syntactic or phrase-based SMT models.

Acknowledgments

We are grateful to the Swiss National Science Foundation (SNSF) for partially funding this work and the research visit to Edinburgh with the COMTIS Sinergia project, n. CRSI22_127510 (see www.idiap.ch/comtis/) and to the three anonymous reviewers for their helpful comments.

References

Shoshana Blum-Kulka. 1986. Shifts of Cohesion and Coherence in Translation. In Juliane House and Shoshana Blum-Kulka, editors, *Interlingual and Intercultural Communication. Discourse and cognition in translation and second language acquisition*, pages 17–35. Narr Verlag, Tübingen, Germany.

Bruno Cartoni, Sandrine Zufferey, Thomas Meyer, and Andrei Popescu-Belis. 2011. How Comparable are Parallel Corpora? Measuring the Distribution of General Vocabulary and Connectives. In *Proceedings of 4th Workshop on Building and Using Comparable Corpora (BUCC)*, pages 78–86, Portland, OR.

Marcello Federico, Nicola Bertoldi, and Mauro Cettolo. 2008. IRSTLM: an Open Source Toolkit for

Handling Large Scale Language Models. In *Proceedings of Interspeech*, Brisbane, Australia.

Najeh Hajlaoui and Andrei Popescu-Belis. 2013. Assessing the Accuracy of Discourse Connective Translations: Validation of an Automatic Metric. In *14th International Conference on Intelligent Text Processing and Computational Linguistics (CICLING)*, Samos, Greece.

Sandra Halverson. 2004. Connectives as a Translation Problem. In H. et al. (Eds.) Kittel, editor, *Encyclopedia of Translation Studies*, pages 562–572. Walter de Gruyter, Berlin/New York.

Silvia Hansen-Schirra, Stella Neumann, and Erich Steiner. 2007. Cohesive Explicitness and Explicitation in an English-German Translation Corpus. *Languages in Contrast*, 7:241–265.

Iustina Ilisei, Diana Inkpen, Gloria Pastor Corpas, and Ruslan Mitkov. 2010. Identifcation of Translationese: A Machine Learning Approach. In A. Gelbukh, editor, *Computational Linguistics and Intelligent Text Processing Lecture Notes in Computer Science*. Springer-Verlag, Berlin, Heidelberg, Germany.

Philipp Koehn, Hieu Hoang, Alexandra Birch, Chris Callison-Burch, Marcello Federico, Nicola Bertoldi, Brooke Cowan, Wade Shen, Christine Moran, Richard Zens, Chris Dyer, Ondrej Bojar, Alexandra Constantin, and Evan Herbs. 2007. Moses: Open Source Toolkit for Statistical Machine Translation. In *Proceedings of 45th Annual Meeting of the Association for Computational Linguistics (ACL), Demonstration Session*, pages 177–180, Prague, Czech Republic.

Philipp Koehn. 2005. Europarl: A Parallel Corpus for Statistical Machine Translation. In *Proceedings of MT Summit X*, pages 79–86, Phuket, Thailand.

Moshe Koppel and Noam Ordan. 2011. Translationese and its Dialects. In *Proceedings of ACL-HLT 2011 (49th Annual Meeting of the ACL: Human Language Technologies*, pages 1318–1326, Portland, OR.

Franz Josef Och and Hermann Ney. 2003. A Systematic Comparison of Various Statistical Alignment Models. *Computational Linguistics*, 29(1):19–51.

Rashmi Prasad, Nikhil Dinesh, Alan Lee, Eleni Miltsakaki, Livio Robaldo, Aravind Joshi, and Bonnie Webber. 2008. The Penn Discourse Treebank 2.0. In *Proceedings of 6th International Conference on Language Resources and Evaluation (LREC)*, pages 2961–2968, Marrakech, Morocco.

Rashmi Prasad, Aravind Joshi, and Bonnie Webber. 2010. Realization of Discourse Relations by Other Means: Alternative Lexicalizations. In *Proceedings of the 23rd International Conference on Computational Linguistics (COLING)*, pages 1023–1031, Beijing, China.

Sandrine Zufferey, Liesbeth Degand, Andrei Popescu-Belis, and Ted Sanders. 2012. Empirical Validations of Multilingual Annotation Schemes for Discourse Relations. In *Proceedings of ISA-8 (8th Workshop on Interoperable Semantic Annotation)*, pages 77–84, Pisa, Italy.

EN conn.	Majority rel.	Tokens	EN conn.	Majority rel.	Tokens
after	Asynchrony	575/577	just as	Synchrony	13/14
also	Conjunction	1735/1746	later	Asynchrony	90/91
although	Contrast	*157/328	meanwhile	Synchrony	148/193
as	Synchrony	543/743	moreover	Conjunction	100/101
as a result	Cause	78/78	nevertheless	Concession	*19/44
as if	Concession	*4/16	nonetheless	Concession	17/27
as long as	Condition	20/24	now that	Cause	20/22
as soon as	Asynchrony	11/20	once	Asynchrony	78/84
because	Cause	854/858	on the other hand	Contrast	35/37
before	Asynchrony	326/326	otherwise	Alternative	22/24
but	Contrast	2427/3308	previously	Asynchrony	49/49
by contrast	Contrast	27/27	separately	Conjunction	73/74
even if	Concession	*41/83	since	Cause	104/184
even though	Concession	72/95	so that	Cause	31/31
finally	Asynchrony	*14/32	still	Concession	83/190
for example	Instantiation	194/196	then	Asynchrony	312/340
for instance	Instantiation	98/98	therefore	Cause	26/26
however	Contrast	355/485	though	Concession	*156/320
if	Condition	1127/1223	thus	Cause	112/112
in addition	Conjunction	165/165	unless	Alternative	94/95
indeed	Conjunction	54/104	until	Asynchrony	140/162
in fact	Restatement	*39/82	when	Synchrony	594/989
instead	Alternative	109/112	while	Contrast	455/781
in turn	Asynchrony	20/30	yet	Contrast	53/101

Table 1: English connectives with a frequency above 20 in the PDTB. Also listed are the level-2 majority relations with the number of tokens out of the total tokens of the connective in the PDTB (counts including the majority relation being part of a composite sense tag). *For some connectives there is no level-2 majority because some instances have only been annotated with level-1 senses. We did not consider the connectives *and* and *or* (too many non-connective occurrences for automatic detection).

Associative Texture is Lost in Translation

Beata Beigman Klebanov and Michael Flor
Educational Testing Service
660 Rosedale Road
Princeton, NJ 08541
{bbeigmanklebanov,mflor}@ets.org

Abstract

We present a suggestive finding regarding the loss of associative texture in the process of machine translation, using comparisons between (a) original and back-translated texts, (b) reference and system translations, and (c) better and worse MT systems. We represent the amount of association in a text using **word association profile** – a distribution of pointwise mutual information between all pairs of content word types in a text. We use the average of the distribution, which we term **lexical tightness**, as a single measure of the amount of association in a text. We show that the lexical tightness of human-composed texts is higher than that of the machine translated materials; human references are tighter than machine translations, and better MT systems produce lexically tighter translations. While the phenomenon of the loss of associative texture has been theoretically predicted by translation scholars, we present a measure capable of quantifying the extent of this phenomenon.

1 Introduction

While most current approaches to machine translation concentrate on single sentences, there is emerging interest in phenomena that go beyond a single sentence and pertain to the whole text being translated. For example, Wong and Kit (2012) demonstrated that repetition of content words is a predictor of translation quality, with poorer translations failing to repeat words appropriately. Gong et al. (2011) and Tiedemann (2010) present caching of translations from earlier sections of a document to facilitate the translation of its later sections.

In scholarship that deals with properties of human translation of literary texts, translation is often rendered as a process that tends to *deform* the original, and a number of particular aspects of deformation have been identified. Specifically, Berman (2000) discusses the problem of *quantitative impoverishment* thus:

> This refers to a lexical loss. Every work in prose presents a certain *proliferation* of signifiers and signifying chains. Great novelist prose is "abundant." These signifiers can be described as *unfixed*, especially as a signified may have a multiplicity of signifiers. For the signified *visage* (face) Arlt employs *semblante*, *rosto* and *cara* without justifying a particular choice in a particular sentence. The essential thing is that *visage* is marked as an important *reality* in his work by the use of three signifiers. The translation that does not respect this multiplicity renders the "visage" of an unrecognizable work. There is a loss, then, since the translation contains fewer signifiers than the original."[1]

While Berman's remarks refer to literary translation, recent work demonstrates its relevance for machine translation, showing that MT systems tend to under-use linguistic devices that are commonly used for repeated reference, such as superordinates or meronyms, although the pattern with synonyms and near-synonyms was not clear cut (Wong and Kit, 2012). Studying a complementary phenomenon of translation of same-lemma lexical items in the source document into a target language, Carpuat and Simard (2012) found that when MT systems produce different target language translations, they are stylistically, syntactically, or semantically inadequate in most cases

[1] italics in the original

(see upper panel of Table 5 therein), that is, diversifying the signifiers appropriately is a challenging task. For recent work on biasing SMT systems towards consistent translations of repeated words, see Ture et al. (2012) and Xiao et al. (2011).

Moving beyond single signifieds, or concepts, Berman faults translations for "the destruction of underlying networks of signification", whereby groups of related words are translated without preserving the relatedness in the target language. While these might be unavoidable in any translation, we show below that machine translation specifically indeed suffers from such a loss (section 3) and that machine translation suffers from it more than the human translations (section 4).

2 Methodology

We define $\mathbf{WAP_T}$ – a **word association profile** of a text T – as the distribution of PMI(x, y) for all pairs of content[2] word types (x, y) ∈T.[3] We estimate PMIs using same-paragraph co-occurrence counts from a large and diverse corpus of about 2.5 billion words: 2 billion words come from the Gigaword 2003 corpus (Graff and Cieri, 2003); an additional 500 million words come from an in-house corpus containing popular science and fiction texts. We further define $\mathbf{LT_T}$ – the **lexical tightness** of a text T – as the average value of the word association profile. All pairs of words in T for which the corpus had no co-occurrence data are excluded from the calculations. We note that the database has very good coverage with respect to the datasets in sections 3-5, with 94%-96% of pairs on average having co-occurrence counts in the database. A more detailed exposition of the notion of a word association profile, including measurements on a number of corpora, can be found in Beigman Klebanov and Flor (2013).

Our prediction is that translated texts would be less lexically tight than originals, and that better translations – either human or machine – would be tighter than worse translations, incurring a smaller amount of association loss.

3 Experiment 1: Back-translation

For the experiment, we selected 20 editorials on the topic of baseball from the New York Times Annotated Corpus.[4] The selected articles had baseball annotated as their sole topic, and ranged from 250 to 750 words in length. We expect these articles to contain a large group of words that reflects vocabulary that is commonly used in discussing baseball and no other systematic subtopics. All articles were translated into French, Spanish, Arabic, and Swedish, and then translated back to English, using the Google automatic translation service. Our goal is to observe the effect of the two layers of translation (out of English and back) on the lexical tightness of the resulting texts.

Since baseball is not a topic that is commonly discussed in the European languages or in Arabic, this is a case where culturally foreign material needs to be rendered in a host (or target) language. This is exactly the kind of situation where we expect deformation to occur – the material is either altered so that is feels more "native" in the host language (domestication) or its foreigness is preserved (foreignization) in that the material lacks associative support in the host language (Venuti, 1995). In the first case, the translation might be associatively adequate *in the host language*, but, being altered, it would produce less culturally precise result when translated back into English. In the second case, the result of translating out of English might already be associatively impoverished *by the standards of the host language*.

The italicized phrases in the previous paragraph underscore the theoretical and practical difficulty in diagnozing domestication or foreignization in translating out of English – an associative model for each of the host languages will be needed, as well as some benchmark of the lexical tightness of native texts written on the given topic against which translations from English could be judged. While the technique of back-translation cannot identify the exact path of association loss – through domestication or foreignization – it can help *establish that association loss has occurred* in at least one or both of the translation processes involved, since the original native English version provides a natural benchmark against which the resulting back-translations can be measured.

To make the phenomenon of association loss more concrete, consider the following sentence:

Original Dave Magadan, the *hard-hitting rookie third baseman* groomed to replace Knight, has been hospitalized.

[2]We part-of-speech tag a text using OpenNLP tagger (http://opennlp.apache.org) and only take into account common and proper nouns, verbs, adjectives, and adverbs.

[3]PMI = Pointwise Mutual Information

[4]LDC2008T19 in LDC catalogue

Arabic Dave Magadan, the *stern rookie 3 baseman* groomed to replace Knight, is in the hospital.[5]

Spanish Dave Magadan, the *strong rookie third baseman* who managed to replace Knight, has been hospitalized.

French Dave Magadan, the *hitting third rookie player* prepared to replace Knight, was hospitalized.

Swedish Dave Magadan, *powerful rookie third baseman* groomed to replace Knight, has been hospitalized.

Observe the translations of the phrase "hard-hitting rookie third baseman." While substituting *strong* and *powerful* for *hard-hitting* might seem acceptable semantically, these terms are not associated with the other baseball terms in the text, whereas *hitting* is highly associated with them:[6] Table 1 shows PMI scores for each of *hitting, stern, strong, powerful* with the baseball terms *rookie* and *baseman*. The French translation got the *hitting*, but substituted the more generic term *player* instead of the baseball-specific *baseman*. As the bottom panel of Table 1 makes clear, while *player* is associated with other baseball terms, the associations are lower than those of *baseman*.

	rookie	baseman	hitting
hitting	3.54	5.29	
stern	0.35	-1.60	
strong	0.54	-0.08	
powerful	-0.62	-0.63	
player	3.95		2.73
baseman	5.11		5.29

Table 1: PMI associations of words introduced in back-translations with baseball terms *rookie, baseman*, and *hitting*.

Table 2 shows the average lexical tightness values across 20 texts for the original version as well as for the back translated versions. The original version is statistically significantly tighter than each of the back translated versions, using 4 applications of t-test for correlated samples, n=20, $p<0.05$ in each case.

[5]We corrected the syntax of all back-translations while preserving the content-word vocabulary choices.

[6]Our tokenizer splits words on hyphens, therefore examples are shown for *hitting* rather than for *hard-hitting*. The point still holds, since *hitting* is a baseball term on its own.

Version	Av. LT	Std. LT	Min. LT	Max. LT
Original	**.953**	.092	.832	1.144
Via Arabic	.875	.093	.747	1.104
Via Spanish	.909	.081	.801	1.069
Via French	.912	.087	.786	1.123
Via Swedish	.931	.099	.796	1.131

Table 2: Average lexical tightness (Av. LT) for the original vs back translated versions, on 20 baseball texts from the New York Times. Standard deviation, minimum, and maximum values are also shown.

4 Experiment 2: Reference vs Machine Translation

We use a part of the dataset used in the NIST Open MT 2008 Evaluation.[7] Our set contains translations of 120 news and web articles from Arabic to English. For each document, there are 4 human reference translations and 17 machine translations by various systems that participated in the benchmark. Table 3 shows the average and standard deviation of lexical tightness values across the 120 texts for each of the four reference translations, each of the 17 MT systems, as well as an average across the four reference translations, and an average across the 17 MT systems. Each of the 17 MT systems is statistically significantly less tight than the average reference human translation (17 applications of the t-test for correlated samples, n=120, $p<0.05$); 12 of the 17 MT systems are statistically significantly less tight than the *least* tight human reference (reference translation #3) at $p<0.05$; the average system translation is statistically significantly less tight that the average human translation at $p<0.05$.

To exemplify a large gap in associative texture between reference and machine translations, consider the following extracts.[8] As the raw MT version (MT-raw) is barely readable, we provide a version where words are re-arranged for readability (MT-read), preserving most of the vocabulary. Since lexical tightness operates on content word types, adding or removing repetitions and function words does not impact the calculation, so we removed or inserted those for the sake of readability

[7]LDC2010T01

[8]The first paragraph of arb-WL-1-154489-7725312#Arabic#system21#c.xml vs arb-WL-1-154489-7725312#Arabic#reference_1#r.xml.

Translation	Av. LT	Std. LT	Min. LT	Max. LT
Ref. 1	.873	.140	.590	1.447
Ref. 2	.851	.124	.636	1.256
Ref. 3	.838	.121	.657	1.177
Ref. 4	.865	.131	.639	1.429
Av. Ref.	.857	.124	.641	1.317
MT 1	.814	.110	.670	1.113
MT 2	.824	.109	.565	1.089
MT 3	.818	.113	.607	1.137
MT 4	.836	.116	.615	1.144
MT 5	.803	.097	.590	1.067
MT 6	.824	.116	.574	1.173
MT 7	.819	.115	.576	1.162
MT 8	.810	.104	.606	1.157
MT 9	.827	.114	.546	1.181
MT 10	.827	.122	.569	1.169
MT 11	.814	.116	.606	1.131
MT 12	.826	.112	.607	1.119
MT 13	.823	.115	.619	1.116
MT 14	.826	.115	.630	1.147
MT 15	.820	.107	.655	1.124
MT 16	.827	.112	.593	1.147
MT 17	.835	.117	.642	1.169
Av. MT	.822	.107	.623	1.106

Table 3: Average lexical tightness (Av. LT) for the reference vs machine translations, on the NIST Open MT 2008 Evaluation Arabic to English corpus. Standard deviation, minimum, and maximum values across the 120 texts are also shown.

in the MT-read version.

MT-raw vision came to me on dream in view of her dream: Arab state to travel to and group of friends on my mission and travel quickly I was with one of the girls seem close to the remaining more than I was happy and you're raised ended === known now

MT-read A vision came to me in a dream. I was to travel quickly to an Arab state with a group of friends on a mission. I was with one of the girls who seemed close to the remaining ones. I was happy and you are raised. It ended. It is known now.

Ref A Dream. My sister came to tell me about a dream she had while she slept. She was saying: I saw you preparing to travel to an Arab country, myself and a group of girlfriends. You were sent on a scholarship abroad, and you were preparing to travel quickly. You were with one of the girls, who appeared to be closer to you than the others, and I was happy and excited because you were traveling. The end. I now know !

The use of *vision* instead of *dream*, *state* instead of *country*, *friends* instead of *girlfriends*, *mission* instead of *scholarship*, *raised* instead of *excited*, along with the complete disapperance of *slept*, *sister*, *preparing*, *abroad*, all contribute to a dramatic loss of associative texture in the MT version. Highly associated pairs like *dream-slept*, *tell-saying*, *girlfriends-girls*, *travel-abroad*, *sister-girls*, *happy-excited*, *travel-traveling* are all missed in the machine translation, while the newly introduced word *raised* is quite unrelated to the rest of the vocabulary in the extract.

5 Experiment 3: Quality of Machine Translation

5.1 System-Level Comparison

In this experiment, we address the following question: Is it the case that when a worse MT system A and a better MT system B translate the same set of materials, B tends to provide more lexically tight translations?

To address this question, we use the Metrics-MATR 2008 development set (Przybocki et al., 2009) from NIST Open MT 2006 evaluation. Eight MT systems were used to translate 25 news articles from Arabic to English, and humans provided scores for translation adequacy on a 1-7 scale. We calculated the average lexical tightness over 25 texts for each of the eigth MT systems, as well as the average translation score for each of the systems. We note that human scores are available per text segments (roughly equivalent to a sentence, 249 segments in total for 25 texts), rather than for whole texts. We first derive a human score for the whole text for a given system by averaging the scores of the system's translations of the different segments of the text. We then derive a human score for an MT system by averaging the scores of its translations of the 25 texts. We found that the average adequacy score of a system is statistically significantly positively correlated with the average lexical tightness that the system's translations exhibit: r=0.630, n=8, df = 6, $p<0.05$.

5.2 Translation-Level Comparison

The same data could be used to answer the question: Is it the case that better translations are lexically tighter? Experiment 2 demonstrated that human reference translations are tighter than machine translations; does the same relationship hold for better vs worse machine translations? To address this question, 25 x 8 = 200 instances of (system, text) pairs can be used, where each has a human score for translation adequacy and a lexical tightness value. Human scores and lexical tightness of a translated text are significantly positively correlated, r=0.178, n=200, p<0.05. Note, however, that this analysis is counfounded by the variation in lexical tightness that exists between texts: As standard deviations and ranges in Tables 2 and 3 make clear, original human texts, as well as reference human translation for different texts, vary in their lexical tightness. Therefore, a lower lexical tightness value can be expected for certain texts even for adequate translations, while for other texts low values of lexical tightness signal a low quality translation. System-level analysis as presented in section 5.1 avoids this confounding, since all systems translated the same set of texts, therefore average tightness values per system are directly comparable.

6 Discussion and Conclusion

We presented a suggestive finding regarding the loss of associative texture in the process of machine translation, using comparisons between (a) original and back-translated texts, (b) reference and system translations, (c) better and worse machine translations. We represented the amount of association in a text using **word association profile** – a distribution of point wise mutual information between all pairs of content word types in a text. We used the average of the distribution, which we term **lexical tightness** – as a single measure of the amount of association in a text. We showed that the lexical tightness of human-composed texts is higher than that of the machine translated materials. While the phenomenon of the loss of associative texture has been theoretically predicted by translation scholars, lexical tightness is a computational measure capable of quantifying the extent of this phenomenon.

Our work complements that of Wong and Kit (2012) in demonstrating the potential utility of discourse-level phenomena to assess machine translations. First, we note that our findings are orthogonal to the main finding in Wong and Kit (2012) regarding loss of cohesion through insufficient word repetition, since our measure looks at pairs of word types, hence disregards repetitions. Second, the notion of pairwise word association generalizes the notion of lexical cohesive devices by looking not only at repeated reference with different lexical items or at words standing in certain semantic relations to each other, but at the whole of the lexical network of the text. Third, differently from the cohesion measure proposed by Wong and Kit (2012), the lexical tightness measure does not depend on lexicographic resources such as WordNet that do not exist in many languages.

References

Beata Beigman Klebanov and Michael Flor. 2013. Word Association Profiles and their Use for Automated Scoring of Essays. In *Proceedings of the Annual Meeting of the Association for Computational Linguistics*, Sofia, Bulgaria, August.

Antoine Berman. 2000. Translation and the Trials of the Foreign (translated from 1985 French original by L. Venuti). In Lawrence Venuti, editor, *The Translation Studies Reader*, pages 276–289. New York: Routledge.

Marine Carpuat and Michel Simard. 2012. The Trouble with SMT Consistency. In *Proceedings of the 7th Workshop on Statistical Machine Translation*, pages 442–449, Montréal, Canada, June. Association for Computational Linguistics.

Zhengxian Gong, Min Zhang, and Guodong Zhou. 2011. Cache-based document-level statistical machine translation. In *Proceedings of the 2011 Conference on Empirical Methods in Natural Language Processing*, pages 909–919, Edinburgh, Scotland, UK., July. Association for Computational Linguistics.

David Graff and Christopher Cieri. 2003. English Gigaword LDC2003T05. Linguistic Data Consortium, Philadelphia.

Mark Przybocki, Kay Peterson, and Sebastien Bronsart. 2009. 2008 NIST metrics for machine translation (MetricsMATR08) development data.

Jörg Tiedemann. 2010. Context adaptation in statistical machine translation using models with exponentially decaying cache. In *Proceedings of the 2010 Workshop on Domain Adaptation for Natural Language Processing*, pages 8–15, Uppsala, Sweden, July. Association for Computational Linguistics.

Ferhan Ture, Douglas W. Oard, and Philip Resnik. 2012. Encouraging consistent translation choices. In *Proceedings of the 2012 Conference of the North American Chapter of the Association for Computational Linguistics: Human Language Technologies*, pages 417–426, Montréal, Canada, June. Association for Computational Linguistics.

Lawrence Venuti. 1995. *The Translator's Invisibilty: A History of Translation*. London & New York: Routledge.

Billy Tak-Ming Wong and Chunyu Kit. 2012. Extending machine translation evaluation metrics with lexical cohesion to document level. In *EMNLP-CoNLL*, pages 1060–1068.

Tong Xiao, Jingbo Zhu, Shujie Yao, and Hao Zhang. 2011. Document-level consistency verification in machine translation. In *Proceedings of the Machine Translation Summit XIII*.

Detecting Narrativity to Improve English to French Translation of Simple Past Verbs

Thomas Meyer
Idiap Research Institute and EPFL
Martigny and Lausanne, Switzerland
thomas.meyer@idiap.ch

Cristina Grisot
University of Geneva
Switzerland
cristina.grisot@unige.ch

Andrei Popescu-Belis
Idiap Research Institute
Martigny, Switzerland
andrei.popescu-belis@idiap.ch

Abstract

The correct translation of verb tenses ensures that the temporal ordering of events in the source text is maintained in the target text. This paper assesses the utility of automatically labeling English Simple Past verbs with a binary discursive feature, narrative vs. non-narrative, for statistical machine translation (SMT) into French. The narrativity feature, which helps deciding which of the French past tenses is a correct translation of the English Simple Past, can be assigned with about 70% accuracy (F1). The narrativity feature improves SMT by about 0.2 BLEU points when a factored SMT system is trained and tested on automatically labeled English-French data. More importantly, manual evaluation shows that verb tense translation and verb choice are improved by respectively 9.7% and 3.4% (absolute), leading to an overall improvement of verb translation of 17% (relative).

1 Introduction

The correct rendering of verbal tenses is an important aspect of translation. Translating to a wrong verbal tense in the target language does not convey the same meaning as the source text, for instance by distorting the temporal order of the events described in a text. Current statistical machine translation (SMT) systems may have difficulties in choosing the correct verb tense translations, in some language pairs, because these depend on a wider-range context than SMT systems consider. Indeed, decoding for SMT is still at the phrase or sentence level only, thus missing information from previously translated sentences (which is also detrimental to lexical cohesion and co-reference).

In this paper, we explore the merits of a discourse feature called *narrativity* in helping SMT systems to improve their translation choices for English verbs in the Simple Past tense (henceforth, SP) into one of the three possible French past tenses. The narrativity feature characterizes each occurrence of an SP verb, either as *narrative* (for ordered events that happened in the past) or *non-narrative* (for past states of affairs). Narrativity is potentially relevant to EN/FR translation because three French past tenses can potentially translate an English Simple Past (SP), namely the *Passé Composé* (PC), *Passé Simple* (PS) or *Imparfait* (IMP). All of them can be correct translations of an EN SP verb, depending on its narrative or non-narrative role.

The narrativity feature can be of use to SMT only if it can be assigned with sufficient precision over a source text by entirely automatic methods. Moreover, a narrativity-aware SMT model is likely to make a difference with respect to baseline SMT only if it is based on additional features that are not captured by, e.g., a phrase-based SMT model. In this study, we use a small amount of manually labeled instances to train a narrativity classifier for English texts. The (imperfect) output of this classifier over the English side of a large parallel corpus will then be used to train a narrativity-aware SMT system. In testing mode, the narrativity classifier provides input to the SMT system, resulting (as we will show below) in improved tense and lexical choices for verbs, and a modest but statistically significant increase in BLEU and TER scores. Overall, the method is similar in substance to our previous work on the combination of a classifier for discourse connectives with an SMT system (Meyer and Popescu-Belis, 2012; Meyer et al., 2012).

The paper is organized as follows. Section 2 exemplifies the hypothesized relation between narrativity and the translations of the English Simple Past into French, along with related work on modeling tense for MT. The automatic labeling experiments are presented in Section 3. Experiments with SMT systems are presented in Section 4, with results from both automatic (4.3) and manual translation scoring (4.4), followed by a discussion of results and suggestions on improving them (Section 5).

2 English Simple Past in Translation

2.1 Role of Narrativity: an Example

The text in Figure 1 is an example taken from the 'newstest 2010' data described in Section 4 below. In this four-sentence discourse, the English verbs, all in Simple Past, express a series of events having occurred in the past, which no longer affect the present. As shown in the French translation by a baseline SMT system (not aware of narrativity), the English SP verbs are translated into the most frequent tense in French, as learned from the parallel data the SMT was trained on.

When looking more closely, however, it appears that the Simple Past actually conveys different temporal and aspectual information. The verbs *offered* and *found* describe actual events that were ordered in time and took place subsequently, whereas *were* and *was* describe states of general nature, not indicating any temporal ordering.

The difference between narrative and non-narrative uses of the English Simple Past is not always captured correctly by the baseline SMT output in this example. The verbs in the first and third sentences are correctly translated into the French PC (one of the two tenses for past narratives in French along with the PS). The verb in the second sentence is also correctly rendered as IMP, in a non-narrative use. However, the verb *was* in the fourth sentence should also have been translated as an IMP, but from lack of sufficient information, it was incorrectly translated as a PC. A non-narrative label could have helped to find the correct verb tense, if it would have been annotated prior to translation.

EN: (1) After a party, I offered [**Narrative**] to throw out a few glass and plastic bottles. (2) But, on Kounicova Ulice, there were [**Non-narrative**] no colored bins to be seen. (3) Luckily, on the way to the tram, I found [**Narrative**] the right place. (4) But it was [**Non-narrative**] overflowing with garbage.

FR from BASELINE MT system: (1) Après un parti, j'**ai proposé** pour rejeter un peu de verre et les bouteilles en plastique. (2) Mais, sur Kounicova Ulice, il n'y **avait** pas de colored bins à voir. (3) Heureusement, sur la manière de le tramway, j'**ai trouvé** la bonne place. (4) Mais il ***a été** débordés avec des ramasseurs.

Figure 1: Example English text from 'newstest 2010' data with narrativity labels and a translation into French from a baseline SMT. The tenses generated in French are, respectively: (1) PC, (2) IMP, (3) PC, (4) PC. The mistake on the fourth one is explained in the text.

2.2 Modeling Past Tenses

The classical view on verb tenses that express past tense in French (PC, PS and IMP) is that both the PC and PS are perfective, indicating that the event they refer to is completed and finished (Martin, 1971). Such events are thus single points in time without internal structure. However, on the one hand, the PC signals an accomplished event (from the aspectual point of view) and thus conveys as its meaning the possible consequence of the event. The PS on the other hand is considered as aspectually unaccomplished and is used in contexts where time progresses and events are temporally ordered, such as narratives.

The IMP is imperfective (as its name suggests), i.e. it indicates that the event is in its preparatory phrase and is thus incomplete. In terms of aspect, the IMP is unaccomplished and provides background information, for instance ongoing state of affairs, or situations that are repeated in time, with an internal structure.

Conversely, in English, the SP is described as having as its main meaning the reference to past tense, and as specific meanings the reference to present or future tenses identified under certain contextual conditions (Quirk et al., 1986). Corblin and de Swart (2004) argue that the SP is aspectually 'transparent', meaning that it applies to all types of events and it preserves their aspectual class.

The difficulty for the MT systems is thus to choose correctly among the three above-mentioned tenses in French, which are all valid possibilities of translating the English SP. When MT systems fail to generate the correct tense in French, several levels of incorrectness may occur, exemplified in Figure 2 with sentences taken from the data used in this paper (see Section 3 and Grisot and Cartoni (2012)).

1. In certain contexts, tenses may be quite interchangeable, which is the unproblematic case for machine translation, depending also on the evaluation measure. In Example 1 from Figure 2, the verb *étaient considérées* (were seen) in IMP has a focus on temporal length which is preserved even if the translated tense is a PC (*ont été considérées*, i.e. have been seen) thanks to the adverb *toujours* (always)).

2. In other contexts, the tense proposed by the MT system can sound strange but remains acceptable. For instance, in Example 2, there is a focus on temporal length with the IMP translation (*voyait*, viewed) but this meaning is not preserved if a PC is used (*a vu*, has viewed) though it can be recovered by the reader.

3. The tense output by an MT system may be grammatically wrong. In Example 3, the PC *a renouvelé* (has renewed) cannot replace the IMP *renouvelaient* (renewed) because of the conflict with the imperfective meaning conveyed by the adverbial *sans cesse* (again and again).

4. Finally, a wrong tense in the MT output can be misleading, if it does not convey the meaning of the source text but remains unnoticed by the reader. In Example 4, using the PC *a été* leads to the interpretation that the person was no longer involved when he died, whereas using IMP *était* implies that he was still involved, which may trigger very different expectations in the mind of the reader (e.g. on the possible cause of the death, or its importance to the peace process).

1. EN: Although the US viewed Musharraf as an agent of change, he has never achieved domestic political legitimacy, and his policies **were seen** as rife with contradictions.
FR: Si les Etats-Unis voient Moucharraf comme un agent de changement, ce dernier n'est jamais parvenu à avoir une légitimité dans son propre pays, où ses politiques ont toujours **été considérées** (PC) / **étaient considérées** (IMP) comme un tissu de contradictions.

2. EN: Indeed, she even persuaded other important political leaders to participate in the planned January 8 election, which she **viewed** as an opportunity to challenge religious extremist forces in the public square.
FR: Benazir Bhutto a même convaincu d'autres dirigeants de participer aux élections prévues le 8 janvier, qu'elle **voyait** (IMP) / **?a vu** (PC) comme une occasion de s'opposer aux extrémistes religieux sur la place publique.

3. EN: The agony of grief which overpowered them at first, **was** voluntarily **renewed**, was sought for, was created again and again...
FR: Elles s'encouragèrent l'une l'autre dans leur affliction, la **renouvelaient** (IMP) / l'***a renouvelé** (PC) volontairement, et sans cesse...

4. EN: Last week a person who **was** at the heart of the peace process passed away.
FR: La semaine passée une personne qui **était** (IMP) / **a été** (PC) au cœur du processus de paix est décédée.

Figure 2: Examples of translations of the English SP by an MT system, differing from the reference translation: (1) unproblematic, (2) strange but acceptable, (3) grammatically wrong (*), and (4) misleading.

2.3 Verb Tenses in SMT

Modeling verb tenses for SMT has only recently been addressed. For Chinese/English translation, Gong et al. (2012) built an n-gram-like sequence model that passes information from previously translated main verbs onto the next verb so that its tense can be more correctly rendered. Tense is morphologically not marked in Chinese, unlike in English, where the verbs forms are modified according to tense (among other factors). With such a model, the authors improved translation by up to 0.8 BLEU points.

Conversely, in view of English/Chinese translation but without implementing an actual translation system, Ye et al. (2007) used a classifier to generate and insert appropriate Chinese aspect markers that in certain contexts have to follow the Chinese verbs but are not present in the English source texts.

For translation from English to German, Gojun and Fraser (2012) reordered verbs in the English source to positions where they normally occur in

German, which usually amounts to a long-distance movement towards the end of clauses. Reordering was implemented as rules on syntax trees and improved the translation by up to 0.61 BLEU points.

In this paper, as SMT training needs a large amount of data, we use an automatic classifier to tag instances of English SP verbs with narrativity labels. The labels output by this classifier are then modeled when training the SMT system.

3 Automatic Labeling of Narrativity

3.1 Data

A training set of 458 and a test set of 118 English SP verbs that were manually annotated with narrativity labels (narrative or non-narrative) was provided by Grisot and Cartoni (2012) (see their article for more details about the data). The training set consists of 230 narrative and 228 non-narrative instances, the test set has 75 narrative instances and 43 non-narrative ones. The sentences come from parallel EN/FR corpora of four different genres: literature, news, parliamentary debates and legislation. For each instance, the English sentence with the SP verb that must be classified, as well as the previous and following sentences, had been given to two human annotators, who assigned a narrative or non-narrative label. To avoid interference with the translation into French, which could have provided clues about the label, the translations were not shown to annotators[1].

Annotators agreed over only 71% of the instances, corresponding to a *kappa* value of only 0.44. As this is at the lower end of the acceptable spectrum for discourse annotation (Carletta, 1996), one of the important questions we ask in this paper is: what can be achieved with this quality of human annotation, in terms of an automatic narrativity classifier (intrinsic performance) and of its use for improving verb translation by SMT (extrinsic evaluation)? It must be noted that instances on which the two annotators had disagreed were resolved (to either narrative or non-narrative) by looking at the French human translation (an acceptable method given that our purpose here is translation into French), thus increasing the quality of the annotation.

[1]The goal was to focus on the narrativity property, regardless of its translation. However, annotations were adjudicated also by looking at the FR translation. For a different approach, considering exclusively the tense in translation, see the discussion in Section 5.

Model	Recall	Prec.	F1	κ
MaxEnt	0.71	0.72	**0.71**	$+\mathbf{0.43}$
CRF	0.30	0.44	0.36	-0.44

Table 1: Performance of MaxEnt and CRF classifiers on narrativity. We report recall, precision, their mean (F1), and the *kappa* value for class agreement.

3.2 Features for Narrativity

The manually annotated instances were used for training and testing a Maximum Entropy classifier using the Stanford Classifier package (Manning and Klein, 2003). We extracted the following features from the sentence containing the verb to classify and the preceding sentence as well, thus modeling a wider context than the one modeled by phrase-based SMT systems. For each verb form, we considered its POS tag and syntactical category, including parents up to the first verbal phrase (VP) parent node, as generated by Charniak and Johnson's constituent parser (2005). This parser also assigns special tags to auxiliary (AUX) and modal verbs (MD), which we include in the features.

We further used a TimeML parser, the Tarsqi Toolkit (Verhagen et al., 2005; Verhagen and Pustejovsky, 2008), which automatically outputs an XML-like structure of the sentence, with a hypothesis on the temporal ordering of the events mentioned. From this structure we extract event markers such as PAST-OCCURRENCE and aspectual information such as STATE.

Temporal ordering is often also signaled by other markers such as adverbials (e.g., *three weeks before*). We manually gathered a list of 66 such temporal markers and assigned them, as an additional feature, a label indicating whether they signal synchrony (e.g., *meanwhile, at the same time*) or asynchrony (e.g., *before, after*).

3.3 Results of Narrativity Labeling

With the above features, we obtained the classification performance indicated in Table 1. The MaxEnt classifier reached 0.71 F1 score, which is similar to the human annotator's agreement level. Moreover, the *kappa* value for inter-class agreement was 0.43 between the classifier and the human annotation, a value which is also close to the *kappa* value for the two human annotators. In a sense, the classifier thus reaches the highest scores that are still meaningful, i.e. those of inter-coder agreement. As a baseline for comparison, the majority class in the test set (the 'narrative' label) would account for 63.56% of correctly classified instances, whereas the classifier correctly labeled 72.88% of all test instances.

For further comparison we built a CRF model (Lafferty et al., 2001) in order to label narrativity in sequence of other tags, such as POS. The CRF uses as features the two preceding POS tags to label the next POS tag in a sequence of words. The same training set of 458 sentences as used above was POS-tagged using the Stanford POS tagger (Toutanova et al., 2003), with the `left3words-distsim` model. We replaced the instances of 'VBD' (the POS tag for SP verbs) with the narrativity labels from the manual annotation. The same procedure was then applied to the 118 sentences of the test set on which CRF was evaluated.

Overall, the CRF model only labeled narrativity correctly at an F1 score of 0.36, while *kappa* had a negative value signaling a weak inverse correlation. Therefore, it appears that the temporal and semantic features used for the MaxEnt classifier are useful and account for the much higher performance of MaxEnt, which is used in the SMT experiments described below.

We further evaluate the MaxEnt classifier by providing in Table 2 the confusion matrix of the automatically obtained narrativity labels over the test set. Labeling non-narrative uses is slightly more prone to errors (32.6% error rate) than narrative ones (24% errors), likely due to the larger number of narratives vs. non-narratives in the training and the test data.

	System		
Reference	**Narr.**	**Non-narr.**	**Total**
Narrative	57	18	75
Non-narr.	14	29	43
Total	71	47	118

Table 2: Confusion matrix for the labels output by the MaxEnt classifier (System) versus the gold standard labels (Reference).

4 SMT with Narrativity Labels

4.1 Method

Two methods to use labels conveying to SMT information about narrativity were explored (though more exist). First, as in our initial studies applied to discourse connectives, the narrativity labels were simply concatenated with the SP verb form in EN (Meyer and Popescu-Belis, 2012) – see Example 2 in Figure 3. Second, we used factored translation models (Koehn and Hoang, 2007), which allow for any linguistic annotation to be considered as additional weighted feature vectors, as in our later studies with connectives (Meyer et al., 2012). These factors are log-linearly combined with the basic features of phrase-based SMT models (phrase translation, lexical and language model probabilities).

To assess the performance gain of narrativity-augmented systems, we built three different SMT systems, with the following names and configurations:

- BASELINE: plain text, no verbal labels.
- TAGGED: plain text, all SP verb forms concatenated with a narrativity label.
- FACTORED: all SP verbs have narrativity labels as source-side translation factors (all other words labeled 'null').

1. BASELINE SMT: on wednesday the čssd declared the approval of next year's budget to be a success. the people's party was also satisfied.

2. TAGGED SMT: on wednesday the čssd declared-**Narrative** the approval of next year's budget to be a success. the people's party was-**Non-narrative** also satisfied.

3. FACTORED SMT: on wednesday the čssd declared|**Narrative** the approval of next year's budget to be a success. the people's party was|**Non-narrative** also satisfied.

Figure 3: Example input sentence from 'newstest 2010' data for three translation models: (1) plain text; (2) concatenated narrativity labels; (3) narrativity as translation factors (the '|null' factors on other words were omitted for readability).

Figure 3 shows an example input sentence for these configurations. For the FACTORED SMT model, both the EN source word and the factor information are used to generate the FR surface target word forms. The tagged or factored annotations are respectively used for the training, tuning and test data as well.

For labeling the SMT data, no manual annotation is used. In a first step, the actual EN SP verbs to be labeled are identified using the Stanford POS tagger, which assigns a 'VBD' tag to each SP verb. These tags are replaced, after feature extraction and execution of the MaxEnt classifier, by the narrativity labels output by the latter. Of course, the POS tagger and (especially) our narrativity classifier may generate erroneous labels which in the end lead to translation errors. The challenge is thus to test the improvement of SMT with respect to the baseline, in spite of the noisy training and test data.

4.2 Data

In all experiments, we made use of parallel English/French training, tuning and testing data from the translation task of the Workshop on Machine Translation (`www.statmt.org/wmt12/`).

- For *training*, we used Europarl v6 (Koehn, 2005), original EN[2] to translated FR (321,577 sentences), with 66,143 instances of SP verbs labeled automatically: 30,452 are narrative and 35,691 are non-narrative.
- For *tuning*, we used the 'newstest 2011' tuning set (3,003 sentences), with 1,401 automatically labeled SP verbs, of which 807 are narrative and 594 non-narrative.
- For *testing*, we used the 'newstest 2010' data (2,489 sentences), with 1,156 automatically labeled SP verbs (621 narrative and 535 non-narrative).

We built a 5-gram language model with SRILM (Stolcke et al., 2011) over the entire FR part of Europarl. Tuning was performed by Minimum Error Rate Training (MERT) (Och, 2003). All translation models were phrase-based using either plain text (possibly with concatenated labels) or factored training as implemented in the Moses SMT toolkit (Koehn et al., 2007).

[2]We only considered texts that were originally authored in English, not translated into it from French or a third-party language, to ensure only proper tenses uses are observed. The relevance of this constraint is discussed for connectives by Cartoni et al. (2011).

4.3 Results: Automatic Evaluation

In order to obtain reliable automatic evaluation scores, we executed three runs of MERT tuning for each type of translation model. With MERT being a randomized, non-deterministic optimization process, each run leads to different feature weights and, as a consequence, to different BLEU scores when translating unseen data.

Table 3 shows the average BLEU and TER scores on the 'newstest 2010' data for the three systems. The scores are averages over the three tuning runs, with resampling of the test set, both provided in the evaluation tool by Clark et al. (2011) (`www.github.com/jhclark/multeval`). BLEU is computed using jBLEU V0.1.1 (an exact reimplementation of NIST's 'mteval-v13.pl' script without tokenization). The Translation Error Rate (TER) is computed with version 0.8.0 of the software (Snover et al., 2006). A t-test was used to compute p values that indicate the significance of differences in scores.

Translation model	BLEU	TER
BASELINE	21.4	61.9
TAGGED	21.3	61.8
FACTORED	21.6*	61.7*

Table 3: Average values of BLEU (the higher the better) and TER (the lower the better) over three tuning runs for each model on 'newstest 2010'. The starred values are significantly better ($p < 0.05$) than the baseline.

In terms of overall BLEU and TER scores, the FACTORED model improves performance over the BASELINE by +0.2 BLEU and -0.2 TER (as lower is better), and these differences are statistically significant at the 95% level. On the contrary, the concatenated-label model (noted TAGGED) slightly decreases the global translation performance compared to the BASELINE. A similar behavior was observed when using labeled connectives in combination with SMT (Meyer et al., 2012).

The lower scores of the TAGGED model may be due to the scarcity of data (by a factor of 0.5) when verb word-forms are altered by concatenating them with the narrativity labels. The small improvement by the FACTORED model of overall scores (such as BLEU) is also related to the scarcity of SP verbs: although their translation is improved, as we will now show, the translation of all other words is not changed by our method, so only a small fraction of the words in the test data are changed.

4.4 Results: Human Evaluation

To assess the improvement specifically due to the narrativity labels, we manually evaluated the FR translations by the FACTORED model for the 207 first SP verbs in the test set against the translations from the BASELINE model. As the TAGGED model did not result in good scores, we did not further consider it for evaluation. Manual scoring was performed along the following criteria for each occurrence of an SP verb, by bilingual judges looking both at the source sentence and its reference translation.

- Is the narrativity label correct? ('correct' or 'incorrect') – this is a direct evaluation of the narrativity classifier from Section 3
- Is the verb tense of the FACTORED model more accurate than the BASELINE one? (noted '+' if improved, '=' if similar, '−' if degraded)
- Is the lexical choice of the FACTORED model more accurate than the BASELINE one, regardless of the tense? (again noted '+' or '=' or '−')
- Is the BASELINE translation of the verb phrase globally correct? ('correct' or 'incorrect')
- Is the FACTORED translation of the verb phrase globally correct? ('correct' or 'incorrect')

Tables 4 and 5 summarize the counts and percentages of improvements and/or degradations of translation quality with the systems FACTORED and BASELINE. The correctness of the labels, as evaluated by the human judges on SMT test data, is similar to the values given in Section 3 when evaluated against the test sentences of the narrativity classifier. As shown in Table 4, the narrativity information clearly helps the FACTORED system to generate more accurate French verb tenses in almost 10% of the cases, and also helps to find more accurate vocabulary for verbs in 3.4% of the cases. Overall, as shown in Table 5, the FACTORED model yields more correct translations of the verb phrases than the BASELINE in 9% of the cases – a small but non-negligible improvement.

Criterion	Rating	N.	%	Δ
Labeling	correct	147	71.0	
	incorrect	60	29.0	
Verb tense	+	35	17.0	
	=	157	75.8	+9.7
	−	15	7.2	
Lexical choice	+	19	9.2	
	=	176	85.0	+3.4
	−	12	5.8	

Table 4: Human evaluation of verb translations into French, comparing the FACTORED model against the BASELINE. The Δ values show the clear improvement of the narrativity-aware factored translation model.

System	Rating	Number	%
BASELINE	correct	94	45.5
	incorrect	113	54.5
FACTORED	correct	113	54.5
	incorrect	94	45.5

Table 5: Human evaluation of the global correctness of 207 translations of EN SP verbs into French. The FACTORED model yields 9% more correct translations than the BASELINE one.

An example from the test data shown in Figure 4 illustrates the improved verb translation. The BASELINE system translates the SP verb *looked* incorrectly into the verb *considérer* (*consider*), in wrong number and its past participle only (*considérés*, plural). The FACTORED model generates the correct tense and number (IMP, *semblait*, singular) and the better verb *sembler* (*look, appear*). This example is scored as follows: the labeling is correct ('yes'), the tense was improved ('+'), the lexical choice was improved too ('+'), the BASELINE was incorrect while the FACTORED model was correct.

5 Discussion and Future Work

When looking in detail through the translations that were degraded by the FACTORED model, some were due to the POS tagging used to find the EN SP verbs to label. For verb phrases made of an auxiliary verb in SP and a past participle (e.g. *was born*), the POS tagger outputs *was*/VBD *born*/VBN. As a consequence, our classifier only considers *was*, as non-narrative, although *was*

EN: tawa hallae **looked|Non-narrative** like many other carnivorous dinosaurs.

FR BASELINE: tawa hallae ***considérés** comme de nombreuses autres carnivores dinosaures.

FR FACTORED: tawa hallae **semblait** comme de nombreux autres carnivores dinosaures.

Figure 4: Example comparison of a baseline and improved factored translation. The '|null' factors in EN were omitted for readability. See the text for a discussion.

born as a whole is a narrative event. This can then result in wrong FR tense translations. For instance, the fragment *nelson mandela was*|Non-narrative *born on* ... is translated as: *nelson mandela *était né en* ..., which in FR is pluperfect tense instead of the correct Passé Composé *est né* as in the reference translation. A method to concatenate such verb phrases to avoid such errors is under work.

A further reason for the small improvements in translation quality might be that factored translation models still operate on rather local context, even when the narrativity information is present. To widen the context captured by the translation model, labeling entire verbal phrase nodes in hierarchical or tree-based syntactical models will be considered in the future. Moreover, it has been shown that it is difficult to choose the optimal parameters for a factored translation model (Tamchyna and Bojar, 2013).

In an alternative approach currently under work, a more direct way to label verb tense is implemented, where a classifier can make use of the same features as those extracted here (in Section 3.2), but its classes are those that directly indicate which target verb tense should be output by the SMT. Thus, not only SP verbs can be considered and no intermediate category such as narrativity (that is more difficult to learn) is needed. The classifier will predict which FR tense should be used depending on the context of the EN verbs, for which the FR tense label can be annotated as above, within a factored translation model. Through word alignment and POS tagging, this method has the additional advantage of providing much more training data, extracted from word alignment of the verb phrases, and can be applied to all tenses, not only SP. Moreover, the approach is likely to learn which verbs are preferably translated with which tense: for instance, the verb *started* is much more likely to become *a commencé* (PC) in FR than to *commençait* (IMP), due to its meaning of a punctual event in time, rather than a continuous or repetitive one.

6 Conclusion

The paper presented a method to automatically label English verbs in Simple Past tense with a binary pragmatic feature, narrativity, which helps to distinguish temporally ordered events that happened in the past ('narrative') from past states of affairs ('non-narrative'). A small amount of manually annotated data, combined with the extraction of temporal semantic features, allowed us to train a classifier that reached 70% correctly classified instances. The classifier was used to automatically label the English SP verbs in a large parallel training corpus for SMT systems. When implementing the labels in a factored SMT model, translation into French of the English SP verbs was improved by about 10%, accompanied by a statistically significant gain of +0.2 BLEU points for the overall quality score. In the future, we will improve the processing of verb phrases, and study a classifier with labels that are directly based on the target language tenses.

Acknowledgments

We are grateful for the funding of this work to the Swiss National Science Foundation (SNSF) under the COMTIS Sinergia Project, n. CRSI22_127510 (see `www.idiap.ch/comtis/`). We would also like to thank the anonymous reviewers for their helpful suggestions.

References

Jean Carletta. 1996. Assessing Agreement on Classification Tasks: The Kappa Statistic. *Computational Linguistics*, 22:249–254.

Bruno Cartoni, Sandrine Zufferey, Thomas Meyer, and Andrei Popescu-Belis. 2011. How Comparable are Parallel Corpora? Measuring the Distribution of General Vocabulary and Connectives. In *Proceedings of 4th Workshop on Building and Using Comparable Corpora (BUCC)*, pages 78–86, Portland, OR.

Eugene Charniak and Mark Johnson. 2005. Coarse-to-fine n-best Parsing and MaxEnt Discriminative

Reranking. In *Proceedings of the 43rd Annual Meeting of the Association for Computational Linguistics (ACL)*, pages 173–180, Ann Arbor, MI.

Jonathan Clark, Chris Dyer, Alon Lavie, and Noah Smith. 2011. Better Hypothesis Testing for Statistical Machine Translation: Controlling for Optimizer Instability. In *Proceedings of ACL-HLT 2011 (46th Annual Meeting of the ACL: Human Language Technologies)*, Portland, OR.

Francis Corblin and Henriëtte de Swart. 2004. *Handbook of French Semantics*. CSLI Publications, Stanford, CA.

Anita Gojun and Alexander Fraser. 2012. Determining the Placement of German Verbs in English-to-German SMT. In *Proceedings of the 13th Conference of the European Chapter of the Association for Computational Linguistics (EACL)*, pages 726–735, Avignon, France.

Zhengxian Gong, Min Zhang, Chew Lim Tan, and Guodong Zhou. 2012. N-Gram-Based Tense Models for Statistical Machine Translation. In *Proceedings of the Joint Conference on Empirical Methods in Natural Language Processing (EMNLP) and Computational Natural Language Learning (CoNLL)*, pages 276–285, Jeju Island, Korea.

Cristina Grisot and Bruno Cartoni. 2012. Une description bilingue des temps verbaux: étude contrastive en corpus. *Nouveaux cahiers de linguistique française*, 30:101–117.

Philipp Koehn and Hieu Hoang. 2007. Factored Translation Models. In *Proceedings of the Joint Conference on Empirical Methods in Natural Language Processing (EMNLP) and Computational Natural Language Learning (CoNLL)*, pages 868–876, Prague, Czech Republic.

Philipp Koehn, Hieu Hoang, Alexandra Birch, Chris Callison-Burch, Marcello Federico, Nicola Bertoldi, Brooke Cowan, Wade Shen, Christine Moran, Richard Zens, Chris Dyer, Ondrej Bojar, Alexandra Constantin, and Evan Herbs. 2007. Moses: Open Source Toolkit for Statistical Machine Translation. In *Proceedings of 45th Annual Meeting of the Association for Computational Linguistics (ACL), Demonstration Session*, pages 177–180, Prague, Czech Republic.

Philipp Koehn. 2005. Europarl: A Parallel Corpus for Statistical Machine Translation. In *Proceedings of MT Summit X*, pages 79–86, Phuket, Thailand.

John Lafferty, Andrew McCallum, and Fernando Pereira. 2001. Conditional Random Fields: Probabilistic Models for Segmenting and Labeling Sequence Data. *The Journal of Machine Learning Research*, 8:693–723.

Christopher Manning and Dan Klein. 2003. Optimization, MaxEnt Models, and Conditional Estimation without Magic. In *Tutorial at HLT-NAACL and 41st ACL conferences*, Edmonton, Canada and Sapporo, Japan.

Robert Martin. 1971. *Temps et aspect: essai sur l'emploi des temps narratifs en moyen français*. Klincksieck, Paris, France.

Thomas Meyer and Andrei Popescu-Belis. 2012. Using Sense-labeled Discourse Connectives for Statistical Machine Translation. In *Proceedings of the EACL 2012 Joint Workshop on Exploiting Synergies between IR and MT, and Hybrid Approaches to MT (ESIRMT-HyTra)*, pages 129–138, Avignon, FR.

Thomas Meyer, Andrei Popescu-Belis, Najeh Hajlaoui, and Andrea Gesmundo. 2012. Machine Translation of Labeled Discourse Connectives. In *Proceedings of the Tenth Biennial Conference of the Association for Machine Translation in the Americas (AMTA)*, San Diego, CA.

Franz Josef Och. 2003. Minimum Error Rate Training in Statistical Machine Translation. In *Proceedings of the 41st Annual Meeting of the Association for Computational Linguistics (ACL)*, pages 160–167, Sapporo, Japan.

Randolph Quirk, Sidney Greenbaum, Geoffrey Leech, and Jan Svartvik. 1986. *A Comprehensive Grammar of the English Language*. Pearson Longman, Harlow, UK.

Matthew Snover, Bonnie Dorr, Richard Schwartz, Linnea Micciulla, and John Makhoul. 2006. A Study of Translation Edit Rate with Targeted Human Annotation. In *Proceedings of the Tenth Biennial Conference of the Association for Machine Translation in the Americas (AMTA)*, Cambridge, MA.

Andreas Stolcke, Jing Zheng, Wen Wang, and Victor Abrash. 2011. SRILM at Sixteen: Update and Outlook. In *Proceedings of the IEEE Automatic Speech Recognition and Understanding Workshop*, Waikoloa, Hawaii.

Aleš Tamchyna and Ondřej Bojar. 2013. No Free Lunch in Factored Phrase-Based Machine Translation. In *Proceedings of the 14th International Conference on Computational Linguistics and Intelligent Text Processing (CICLING)*, Samos, Greece.

Kristina Toutanova, Dan Klein, Christopher Manning, and Yoram Singer. 2003. Feature-rich Part-of-Speech Tagging with a Cyclic Dependency Network. In *Proceedings of Human Language Technology Conference and the North American Chapter of the Association for Computational Linguistics (HLT-NAACL)*, pages 252–259, Edmonton, CA.

Marc Verhagen and James Pustejovsky. 2008. Temporal Processing with the TARSQI Toolkit. In *Proceedings of the 22nd International Conference on Computational Linguistics (COLING), Companion volume: Demonstrations*, pages 189–192, Manchester, UK.

Marc Verhagen, Inderjeet Mani, Roser Sauri, Jessica Littman, Robert Knippen, Seok Bae Jang, Anna Rumshisky, John Phillips, and James Pustejovsky. 2005. Automating Temporal Annotation with TARSQI. In *Proceedings of the 43th Annual Meeting of the Association for Computational Linguistics (ACL), Demo Session*, pages 81–84, Ann Arbor, USA.

Yang Ye, Karl-Michael Schneider, and Steven Abney. 2007. Aspect Marker Generation for English-to-Chinese Machine Translation. In *Proceedings of MT Summit XI*, pages 521–527, Copenhagen, Danmark.

Machine Translation with Many Manually Labeled Discourse Connectives

Thomas Meyer
Idiap Research Institute and EPFL
Martigny and Lausanne, Switzerland
thomas.meyer@idiap.ch

Lucie Poláková
Institute of Formal and Applied Linguistics
Faculty of Mathematics and Physics
Charles University in Prague
Prague, Czech Republic
polakova@ufal.mff.cuni.cz

Abstract

The paper presents machine translation experiments from English to Czech with a large amount of manually annotated discourse connectives. The gold-standard discourse relation annotation leads to better translation performance in ranges of 4–60% for some ambiguous English connectives and helps to find correct syntactical constructs in Czech for less ambiguous connectives. Automatic scoring confirms the stability of the newly built discourse-aware translation systems. Error analysis and human translation evaluation point to the cases where the annotation was most and where less helpful.

1 Introduction

Recently, research in statistical machine translation (SMT) has renewed interest in the fact that for a variety of linguistic phenomena one needs information from a longer-range context. Current statistical translation models and decoding algorithms operate at the sentence and/or phrase level only, not considering already translated context from previous sentences. This local distance is in many cases too restrictive to correctly model lexical cohesion, referential expressions (noun phrases, pronouns), and discourse markers, all of which relate to the sentence(s) before the one to be translated.

Discourse relations between sentences are often conveyed by explicit discourse connectives (DC), such as *although, because, but, since, while*. DCs play a significant role in coherence and readability of a text. Likewise, if a wrong connective is used in translation, the target text can be fully incomprehensible or not conveying the same meaning as was established by the discourse relations in the source text. In English, about 100 types of such explicit connectives have been annotated in the Penn Discourse TreeBank (PDTB, see Section 4), signaling discourse relations such as temporality or contrast between two spans of text. Depending on the set of relations used, there can be up to 130 such relations and combinations thereof. Discourse relations can also be present implicitly (inferred from the context), without any explicit marker being present. Although annotation for implicit DCs exists as well, we only deal with explicit DCs in this paper. DCs are difficult to translate mainly because a same English connective can signal different discourse relations in different contexts and when the target language has either different connectives according to the source relations signaled or uses different lexical or syntactical constructs in place of the English connective.

In this paper, we present MT experiments from English (EN) to Czech (CZ) with a large amount of *manually* annotated DCs. The corpus, the parallel Prague Czech-English Dependency Treebank (PCEDT) (Section 4), is directly usable for MT experiments: the entire discourse annotation in EN is paralleled with a human CZ translation. This means that we can build and evaluate, against the CZ reference, a translation system, that learns from the EN gold standard discourse relations. These then have no distortion from wrongly labeled connectives as it is given in related work (Section 3) where automatic classifiers have been used to label the connectives with a certain error rate. Furthermore, we can use the sense labels for 100 types of EN connectives, whereas related work only focused on a few highly ambiguous connectives that are especially problematic for translation.

The paper starts by illustrating difficult translations involving connectives (Section 2) and discusses related work in Section 3. The resources and data used are introduced in Section 4. The MT experiments are explained in Section 5 and automatic evaluation is given in Section 6. We further provide a detailed manual evaluation and error analysis for the CZ translations generated by our SMT systems (Section 7). Future work described in Section 8 concludes the paper.

2 Motivation

The following example shows a CZ translation of the English DC *meanwhile*. The previous sentences to the example were about other computer producers expected to report disappointing financial results. The interpretation of *meanwhile* and the discourse relation (or sense) signaled is therefore CONTRASTIVE and **not** TEMPORAL:

> **SOURCE**: Apple Computer Inc., **meanwhile**<COMPARISONCONTRAST>, is expected to show improved earnings for the period ended September.
> **BASELINE**: Společnost Apple Computer Inc., **mezitím** by měla ukázat lepší příjmy za období končící v září.
> **SYSTEM2**: Společnost Apple Computer Inc., **naopak** by měla ukázat lepší příjmy za období končící v září.

A baseline SMT system for EN/CZ generated the incorrect CZ connective *mezitím* which signals a temporal relation only. The translation marked SYSTEM2 in the example was output by one of the systems we trained on manual DC annotations (cf. Section 5). The system correctly generated the CZ connective *naopak* signaling a contrastive sense. The example sentence is taken from the Wall Street Journal corpus, section 2365. The sense tag for *meanwhile* was manually annotated in the Penn Discourse TreeBank, see Section 4.

3 Related Work

The disambiguation of DCs can be seen as a special form of Word Sense Disambiguation (WSD), that has been applied to SMT for content words with slight improvements to translation quality (Chan et al., 2007; Carpuat and Wu, 2007). DCs however form a class of procedural function words that relate text spans from an arbitrarily long context and their disambiguation needs features from that longer-range context. Only few studies address function word disambiguation for SMT: Chang et al. (2009) disambiguate a multifunctional Chinese particle for Chinese/English translation and Ma et al. (2011) use tagging of English collocational particles for translation into Chinese. Lexical cohesion at the document level has recently also come into play, with studies on lexical consistency in SMT (Carpuat, 2009; Carpuat and Simard, 2012), topic modeling applied to SMT (Eidelman et al., 2012) or decoding with document-wide features (Hardmeier et al., 2012). A recently published article summarizes most of the work on SMT with the broader perspective of discourse, lexical cohesion and coreference (Hardmeier, 2013).

For discourse relations and DCs especially, more and more annotated resources have become available in several languages, such as English (Prasad et al., 2008), French (Péry-Woodley et al., 2009; Danlos et al., 2012), German (Stede, 2004), Arabic (AlSaif, 2012), Chinese (Zhou and Xue, 2012) and Czech (Mladová et al., 2009). These resources however remain mostly monolingual, i.e. translations or parallel texts in other languages do normally not exist. This makes these resources not directly usable for MT experiments.

Recent work has shown that more adequate and coherent translations can be generated for English/French when ambiguous connectives in the source language are annotated with the discourse relation they signal (Popescu-Belis et al., 2012). SMT systems for European language pairs are most often trained on Europarl corpus data (Koehn, 2005), where only a small amount of discourse-annotated instances is available (8 connectives with about 300-500 manual annotations each). Meyer and Popescu-Belis (2012) therefore used these few examples to train automatic classifiers that introduce the sense labels for the connectives in the entire English text of the Europarl corpus. Although these classifiers are state-of-the-art, they can have an error rate of up to 30% when labeling unseen instances of connectives. The discourse-aware SMT systems nevertheless improved about 8-10% of the connective translations. When integrating into SMT directly the small manually-labeled data, without training classifiers, hardly any translation improvement was measurable, cf. (Meyer and Popescu-Belis, 2012).

4 The Parallel Prague Czech-English Dependency Treebank

With the English-Czech parallel text provided in the Prague Czech-English Dependency Treebank 2.0 (PCEDT) (Hajič et al., 2011)[1], comes a human CZ translation of the entire Wall Street Journal Corpus in EN (WSJ, sections 00-24, approxi-

[1]http://www.ldc.upenn.edu/Catalog/catalogEntry.jsp?catalogId=LDC2012T08

mately 50k sentences).

The syntactical annotation of WSJ, the Penn TreeBank (Marcus et al., 1993), has been followed by a discourse annotation project, the Penn Discourse TreeBank (PDTB) (Prasad et al., 2008), over the same sections of the corpus. In the PDTB version 2.0, 18,459 instances of explicit DCs, among other discourse-related phenomena (implicit relations, alternative lexicalizations), are labeled along with the text spans they connect (discourse arguments) and the discourse relation they signal (sense tags).

The sense tags are organized in a three-level sense hierarchy with four top semantic classes, 16 sub-senses on the second and further 23 sub-senses on the third hierarchy level. The annotators were not forced to make the finest distinction (on the sub-sense level). A token can also be annotated with two senses, forming a composite sense with a label combination from wherever in the hierarchy, resulting in 129 theoretically possible distinct sense tags (see Section 5 for the sense levels we use). For the latter reason, some of the sense labels are very scarcely used and although they make for important and fine-grained distinctions in English, this granularity level might not be useful for translation, where only certain ambiguities have to be resolved to obtain a correct target language connective, see Section 7.

The PCEDT is a 1:1 sentence-aligned parallel resource with a manual multilayer dependency analysis of both original Penn TreeBank-WSJ texts and their translations to Czech. Despite the manually annotated parallel dependency trees which are very valuable in other linguistic studies, for translation we only used the plain CZ texts provided with the treebank.

5 Experimental Setup

In the following, we describe a series of SMT experiments that made direct use of the EN/CZ text as provided with the PCEDT. The SMT models were all phrase-based and trained with the Moses decoder (Koehn et al., 2007), either on plain text for the BASELINE or on text where the EN connective word-forms have been concatenated with the PDTB sense labels. All texts have been tokenized and lowercased with the Moses tools before training SMT. In future work, we will build factored translation models (Koehn and Hoang, 2007) as well, as this would reduce the label scarcity that was likely a problem when just concatenating word-forms and labels (see Sections 7 and 8).

For SYSTEM1 in the following, we inserted, into the English side of the PCEDT data, the full sense labels from the PDTB, which can be, as already mentioned, as detailed as containing 3 sense levels and allowing for composite tags (where annotators chose that two senses hold at the same time). SYSTEM1 therefore operates on a total of 63 distinct and observed sense tags for all DCs.

For SYSTEM2, we reduced the sense labels to contain only senses from PDTB sense hierarchy level 2 and 1, not allowing for composite senses, i.e. for those instances that were annotated with two senses we discarded the secondary (but not less important) sense. This reduced the set of senses for SYSTEM2 to 22.

The procedure is exemplified in the example below with an EN sentence 1 (WSJ section 2300) containing a complex PDTB sense tag that has been kept for SYSTEM1. For SYSTEM2 we have reduced the sense of *when* to: <CONTINGENCYCONDITIONGENERAL>. Sentence 2 (WSJ section 2341) contains two already simplified sense tags. The original PDTB sense tags for *meanwhile* and *as* were respectively <COMPARISONCONTRASTJUXTAPOSITION> and <CONTINGENCYPRAGMATICCAUSE-JUSTIFICATION>, where JUXTAPOSITION and JUSTIFICATION were dropped because they stem from the third level of the PDTB sense hierarchy:

> **1.** Selling snowballed because of waves of automatic "stop-loss" orders, which are triggered by computer **when**<CONTINGENCYCONDITIONGENERAL-TEMPORALASYNCHRONOUSSUCCESSION> prices fall to certain levels.
> **2. Meanwhile**<COMPARISONCONTRAST>, analysts said Pfizer's recent string of lackluster quarterly performances continued, **as**<CONTINGENCYPRAGMATICCAUSE> earnings in the quarter were expected to decline by about 5%.

In order to build SMT systems of reasonable quality, we still need to combine the PCEDT texts (50k sentences) with other resources such as the EN/CZ parts of the Europarl corpus. This results in a mixture of labeled and unlabeled DCs in the data and estimates might be noisy. We however also checked system performance on the PDTB test set (section 23) with labeled DCs only (see Section 6) for which the unlabeled ones in the model do not pose a problem, as they are not considered as valid target phrases by the SMT decoder. The following list gives an overview of the data used to build three SMT systems. No modifications have been done to the texts of the BASELINE system, that uses exactly the same amount of sentences, but no sense labels.

- BASELINE: no tags for connectives
- SYSTEM1: complex PDTB sense tags
- SYSTEM2: simplified PDTB sense tags
- training: Europarlv7 (645,155 sentences) + PDTB sections 02-21 (41,532 sentences; 15,402 connectives)
- tuning: newstest2011 (3,003 sentences) + PDTB sections 00,01,22,24 (5,260 sentences; 2,134 connectives)
- testing: newstest2012 (3,001 sentences) + PDTB section 23 (2,416 sentences; 923 connectives)[2]

The language model, the same for BASELINE, SYSTEM1 and SYSTEM2, was built using SRILM (Stolcke et al., 2011) with 5-grams over Europarl and the news data sets 2007-2011 in CZ, as distributed by the Workshop on Machine Translation[3]. All systems were tuned by MERT (Och, 2003) as implemented in Moses.

6 Automatic Evaluation

Most automatic MT scoring relies on n-gram matching of a system's candidate translation against (usually) only one human reference translation. For DCs therefore, automatic scores do not reveal much of a system's performance, as often only one or two words, i.e. the DC is changed. When a candidate translation however contains a more accurate and correct connective, the translation output is often more coherent and readable than the baseline's output, see Section 7.

Automatic evaluation has been done using the MultEval tool, version 0.5.1 (Clark et al., 2011). The BLEU scores are computed by jBLEU V0.1.1 (an exact reimplementation of NIST's mteval-v13.pl without tokenization). Table 1 provides an overview of the BLEU scores for the BASELINE and systems 1 and 2 on the full test set (newstest2012 + PDTB section 23), and on PDTB section 23 only, the latter containing 2,416 sentences and 923 labeled DCs.

In order to gain reliable automatic evaluation scores, we executed 5 runs of MERT for each translation model configuration. MERT is implemented as a randomized, non-deterministic optimization process, so that each run leads to different feature weights and as a consequence, to different BLEU scores when translating unseen text. The scores from the 5 runs were then averaged and with a t-test we calculated the confidence p-values for the score differences. When these are below 0.05, they confirm that it is statistically likely, that such scores would occur again in other tuning runs. In terms of BLEU, neither SYSTEM1 nor SYSTEM2 therefore performs significantly better or worse than the BASELINE.

In order to show how little the DC labeling actually affects the BLEU score, we randomized all connective sense tags in PDTB test section 23 and translated again 5 times (with the weights from each tuning run) with both, SYSTEM1 and SYSTEM2. With randomized labels, both systems perform statistically significantly worse ($p = 0.01$, marked with a star in Table 1) than the BASELINE, but only with an average performance loss of -0.6 BLEU points. Note that some sense tags might still have been correct due to randomization.

Test set	System	BLEU
nt2012 + PDTB 23	BASELINE	17.6
	SYSTEM1	17.6
	SYSTEM2	17.6
PDTB 23	BASELINE	21.4
	SYSTEM1	21.4
	SYSTEM2	21.4
PDTB 23 random	SYSTEM1	20.8*
	SYSTEM2	20.8*

Table 1: BLEU scores when testing on the combined test set (newstest2012 + PDTB 23); on PDTB section 23 only (2416 sentences, 923 connectives); and when randomizing the sense tags (PDTB 23 random), for the BASELINE system and the two systems using PDTB connective labels: SYSTEM1: complex labels, SYSTEM2: simplified labels. When testing on randomized sense labels (PDTB 23 random), the BLEU scores are statistically significantly lower than the ones on the correctly labeled test set (PDTB 23), which is indicated by starred values.

Automatic MT scoring does therefore not reveal actual changes in translation quality due to DC usage. In the next section, we manually analyze

[2]Note that this PDTB section division for training, development and testing is the same as is used for automatic classification experiments, as recommended in the PDTB annotation manual.

[3]http://www.statmt.org/wmt12/

samples of the translation output by SYSTEM2 that reached the highest scores observed in some of the single tuning runs before averaging.

7 Manual Evaluation and Error Analysis

Two human judges went both through two random samples of SYSTEM2 translations from WSJ section 23, namely sentences 1-300 and 1000-2416. In these sentences, there were 630 observed connectives. The judges counted the translations that were better, equal and worse in terms of the DCs as output by SYSTEM2 versus the BASELINE system. We then summarized the counts over the two samples and give the scores as $\Delta(\%)$ in Table 2. To further test if we just had bad samples, the judges went through another set of translations (1024–1138), containing 50 DCs, for which the counts are summarized in Table 2 as well. A translation was counted as being correct when it generated a valid CZ connective for the corresponding context, without grading the rest of the sentences.

Overall, it was found that the number of better translations is only slightly higher for SYSTEM2 than the ones from the BASELINE system. The vast majority of DCs was translated correctly by both the BASELINE and SYSTEM2, and in very few cases, both systems translated the DCs incorrectly.

SYSTEM2 appeared to systematically repeat one mistake, namely translating the very frequent connective *but* preferably with *jenže*, which is correct but rare in CZ (the primary and default equivalent for *but* in CZ is *ale*). This 'mis-learning' likely happened to a frequent correspondence of *but–jenže* in the SMT training data, which then does not necessarily scale to and be of appropriate style in the testing data. If one disregards these occurrences, SYSTEM2 translates between about 8 and 20% of all connectives better than the BASELINE (discounted percentages for *jenže* in Table 2). The results seem therefore to be dependent on the parts of the test set evaluated and the DCs occurring in them.

The only slight quantitative improvements and cases were SYSTEM2 performed worse are most likely due to the overall scarcity of the PDTB sense tags (cf. Section 4). Especially for SYSTEM1 but to some extent also for SYSTEM2, rare sense tags such as CONTINGENCYPRAGMATICCAUSE might not be seen often or even not at all in the SMT training data and therefore not be learned appropriately to provide good translations for the test data. In relation to that, simply concatenating the sense tags onto the connective word-forms leads to scarcity of the latter, whereas other ways to include linguistic labels in SMT, such as factored translation models, would account for the labels as additional translation features, which will be investigated in future work (Section 8).

In the following, we analyze cases where SYSTEM2 translates the connectives better and more appropriately than the BASELINE. These cases include highly ambiguous connectives, temporal DCs with verbal *ing*-forms and conditionals.

In general, for the very ambiguous EN connectives (e.g. *as, when, while)*, disambiguated for SYSTEM2 with the PDTB sense tags, we indeed obtained more accurate translations than those generated by the BASELINE. One of the human judges had a close look at 25 randomly sampled instances of *as*, taken from the manually evaluated sets mentioned above. In these test cases, 68% of all occurrences of *as* were better translated by SYSTEM2 and only 4% of the translations were degraded when compared to the BASELINE. For details, see Table 3[4].

In the following translation example (WSJ section 2365), and often elsewhere, the BASELINE system treats the connective *as* as a preposition *jako* with the meaning *She worked as a teacher.* This frequent interpretation seems to be learned quite reasonably from the SMT training data, it is however incorrect where *as* actually functions as a DC. SYSTEM2, in agreement with the tagging, then correctly generates the causal connective *protože*:

> **SOURCE**: In the occupied lands, underground leaders of the Arab uprising rejected a U.S. plan to arrange Israeli-Palestinian talks **as**<CONTINGENCYCAUSE> Shamir opposed holding such discussions in Cairo.
> **BASELINE**: *Na okupovaných územích, podzemní vůdců arabských povstání odmítl americký plán uspořádat izraelsko-palestinské rozhovory **jako** Šamira proti pořádání takových diskusí v Káhiře.
> **SYSTEM2**: Na okupovaných územích, podzemní vůdců arabského povstání odmítl americký plán uspořádat izraelsko-palestinské rozhovory, **protože** Šamira proti pořádání takových diskusí v Káhiře.

DCs can also be translated to other syntactical constructs available in the target language that convey the same discourse relation without any

[4]We included simple occurrences only, i.e. not compound connectives like *as if, as soon as* or translations were the connective was dropped. In the PDTB, *as* can have up to 17 distinct senses, ranging from temporal, causal to concessive relations.

Configuration	Δ(%) vs. BASELINE Improved	Equal	Degraded	Total (%)
sentences 1–300 / 1000–2416 630 labeled DCs				
SYSTEM2	7.9	75.2	9.4	92.5
not counting 25 x *but–jenže*	8.2	80.3	4.0	92.5
both systems wrong				7.5
				100
sentences 1024–1138 50 labeled DCs				
SYSTEM2	16	76	6	98
not counting 2 x *but–jenže*	19	77	2	98
both systems wrong				2
				100

Table 2: Performance of SYSTEM2 (simplified PDTB tags) when manually counting for improved, equal and degraded translations compared to the BASELINE, in samples from the PDTB section 23 test set.

explicit DC. For EN/CZ this occurs for DCs such as *before/after/since* + Verb in Present Continuous. In CZ, these either should be rendered as a verbal clause or a nominalization. We accounted for translations as being well-formed, if the SMT systems generated one of these possibilities correctly, i.e. not only the connective/preposition but also the verb/noun. In CZ, it must be decided between using a preposition (e.g. *před*) or a connective (e.g. *než*). A good translation would for example be: *before climbing* = PREP+NP or DC+V, and a bad translation: *before climbing* = PREP+V/ADJ or DC+NP. The following example (WSJ section 2381) is a SYSTEM2 output where the sense tag in English helped to translate the connective *before* more correctly by DC+V, whereas the BASELINE renders this wrongly by using PREP+ADJ:

> **SOURCE**: Mr. Weisman predicts stocks will appear to stabilize in the next few days **before**<TemporalAsynchronous> declining again, trapping more investors.
> **BASELINE**: *Pan Weisman předpovídá, že akcie budou stabilizovat v příštích několika dnech před/**PREP** klesajícím/**ADJ** opět odchytu více investorů.
> **SYSTEM2**: Pan Weisman předpovídá, že akcie bude stabilizovat, jak se zdá, v příštích několika dní, než/**DC** opět klesat/**V**, zablokování více investorů.

A further difficult case in CZ is the binding of conditionals with personal pronouns, e.g. *if I = kdybych*, *if you = kdybys*, *if he/she = kdyby* etc. In the following example (WSJ section 2386), the BASELINE system completely missed to render the personal pronoun (but still generated the correct conditional connective *if–pokud*), whereas SYSTEM2 outputs the much better *if I–kdybych*. However, apart from the better connective, SYSTEM2's translation is worse than the BASELINE's, because the first verb form is misconjugated and the second verb (*will take*) is missing:

> **SOURCE**: **If**<ContingencyCondition> I sell now, I'll take a big loss.
> **BASELINE**: ***Pokud** chtěl prodat, teď budu brát s velkou ztrátou.
> **LIT.**: If he-wanted to-sell, now I-will take with big-Instrumental loss-Instrumental.
> **SYSTEM2**: **Kdybych** se nyní prodávají, se z tohohle velkou ztrátu.
> **LIT.**: If-I themselves-ReflexPron now they-are selling, ReflexPron out-of this big-Accusative loss-Accusative.

From the automatic and manual translation evaluation, we conclude that using the sense tags for *all* 100 connectives in EN is not the most appropriate method, and that only certain connectives such as *as, when, while, yet* and a few others are very problematic in translation due to the many discourse relations they can signal. In future work, we will therefore analyze in more detail which connectives and which sense labels from the PDTB should actually be included in the data to train SMT.

BASELINE	SYSTEM2	occ.	PDTB
jak	když	1	SY
jak	**když**	1	SY
jelikož	jelikož	1	CA
neboť	neboť	1	CA
protože	protože	2	SY/CO; CA
a	protože	1	SY/CO
aby	když	1	SY
jak	když	1	SY
jak	protože	1	CA
jako	protože	4	SY/CO; CA
jako	když	5	SY; ASY; CA
jako	kdy	2	SY
protože	když	1	SY
že	když	1	SY
jako	**jak**	1	SY
jako	**poté, co**	1	SY
Total		25	
SYS2 +		68%	
SYS2 =		20%	
SYS2 –		4%	
both –		8%	

Table 3: Translation outputs for the EN connective *as*, which was translated more correctly by SYSTEM2 thanks to the disambiguating sense tags compared to the BASELINE that often just produces the prepositional *as – jako*. The erroneous translations are marked in bold. The PDTB sense tags indicate the meaning of the CZ translations and are encoded as follows: Synchrony (Sy), Asynchrony (Asy), Contingency (Co), Cause (Ca).

8 Conclusion

We presented experiments for EN/CZ SMT with a large amount of hand-labeled discourse connectives that are disambiguated in the source language and training material for MT systems by their sense tags or discourse relations they signal. This leads to improved translations in cases where the source DC is highly ambiguous or where the target language uses other syntactical constructs than a connective to convey the discourse relation.

Using all 100 types of EN DCs in the corpus and/or all the detailed sense tags from the manual annotation most probably lead to the only very slight improvements for the discourse-aware systems when measured quantitatively over the whole test sets. In future work we plan to more thoroughly analyze which connectives need to be disambiguated at which sense granularity level before implementing them into an SMT system.

For label implementation there also are other ways worth examining, such as factored translation models that handle the supplementary linguistic information as separate features and alternative decoding paths.

Acknowledgments

We are grateful for the funding of this work to the Swiss National Science Foundation (SNSF) under the COMTIS Sinergia project, n. CRSI22_127510 (see `www.idiap.ch/comtis/`), to the Grant Agency of the Czech Republic (project n. P406/12/0658) and to the SVV of the Charles University (project n. 267 314). We would like to thank Lenka Sándor for her help with manual translation evaluation.

References

Amal AlSaif. 2012. *Human and Automatic Annotation of Discourse Relations for Arabic*. Ph.D. thesis, University of Leeds.

Marine Carpuat and Michel Simard. 2012. The Trouble with SMT Consistency. In *Proceedings of the 7th Workshop on Statistical Machine Translation (WMT)*, pages 442–449, Montreal, Canada.

Marine Carpuat and Dekai Wu. 2007. Improving Statistical Machine Translation using Word Sense Disambiguation. In *Proceedings of Joint Conference on Empirical Methods in Natural Language Processing (EMNLP) and Computational Natural Language Learning (CoNLL)*, pages 61–72, Prague, Czech Republic.

Marine Carpuat. 2009. One Translation per Discourse. In *Proceedings of the Workshop on Semantic Evaluations: Recent Achievements and Future Directions (SEW)*, pages 19–27, Singapore.

Yee Seng Chan, Hwee Tou Ng, and David Chiang. 2007. Word Sense Disambiguation Improves Statistical Machine Translation. In *Proceedings of the 45th Annual Meeting of the Association of Computational Linguistics (ACL)*, pages 33–40, Prague, Czech Republic.

Pi-Chuan Chang, Dan Jurafsky, and Christopher D. Manning. 2009. Disambiguating 'DE' for Chinese-English Machine Translation. In *Proceedings of the Fourth Workshop on Statistical Machine Translation at the 12th Meeting of the European Chapter of the Association for Computational Linguistics (EACL)*, Athens, Greece.

Jonathan Clark, Chris Dyer, Alon Lavie, and Noah Smith. 2011. Better Hypothesis Testing for Statistical Machine Translation: Controlling for Optimizer Instability. In *Proceedings of ACL-HLT 2011 (46th Annual Meeting of the ACL: Human Language Technologies)*, Portland, OR.

Laurence Danlos, Diégo Antolinos-Basso, Chloé Braud, and Charlotte Roze. 2012. Vers le FDTB : French Discourse Tree Bank. In *Actes de la conférence conjointe JEP-TALN-RECITAL 2012, volume 2: TALN*, pages 471–478, Grenoble, France.

Vladimir Eidelman, Jordan Boyd-Graber, and Philip Resnik. 2012. Topic Models for Dynamic Translation Model Adaptation. In *Proceedings of ACL 2012 (50th Annual Meeting of the Association for Computational Linguistics*, pages 115–119, Jeju, Republic of Korea.

Jan Hajič, Eva Hajičová, Jarmila Panevová, Petr Sgall, Silvie Cinková, Eva Fučíková, Marie Mikulová, Petr Pajas, Jan Popelka, Jiří Semecký, Jana Šindlerová, Jan Štěpánek, Josef Toman, Zdeňka Urešová, and Zdeněk Žabokrtský. 2011. Prague Czech-English Dependency Treebank 2.0. Institute of Formal and Applied Linguistics, Charles University, Prague, Czech Republic.

Christian Hardmeier, Joakim Nivre, and Jörg Tiedemann. 2012. Document-Wide Decoding for Phrase-Based Statistical Machine Translation. In *Proceedings of the Conference on Empirical Methods in Natural Language Processing and Natural Language Learning (EMNLP-CoNLL)*, Jeju, Korea.

Christian Hardmeier. 2013. Discourse in Statistical Machine Translation. *DISCOURS*, 11:1–29.

Philipp Koehn and Hieu Hoang. 2007. Factored Translation Models. In *Proceedings of the Joint Conference on Empirical Methods in Natural Language Processing (EMNLP) and Computational Natural Language Learning (CONLL)*, pages 868–876, Prague, Czech Republic.

Philipp Koehn, Hieu Hoang, Alexandra Birch, Chris Callison-Burch, Marcello Federico, Nicola Bertoldi, Brooke Cowan, Wade Shen, Christine Moran, Richard Zens, Chris Dyer, Ondrej Bojar, Alexandra Constantin, and Evan Herbs. 2007. Moses: Open Source Toolkit for Statistical Machine Translation. In *Proceedings of 45th Annual Meeting of the Association for Computational Linguistics (ACL), Demonstration Session*, pages 177–180, Prague, Czech Republic.

Philipp Koehn. 2005. Europarl: A Parallel Corpus for Statistical Machine Translation. In *Proceedings of MT Summit X*, pages 79–86, Phuket, Thailand.

Jianjun Ma, Degen Huang, Haixia Liu, and Wenfeng Sheng. 2011. POS Tagging of English Particles for Machine Translation. In *Proceedings of the Thirteenth Machine Translation Summit*, pages 57–63, Xiamen, China.

Mitchell P. Marcus, Beatrice Santorini, and Mary Ann Marcinkiewicz. 1993. Building a Large Annotated Corpus of English: The Penn Treebank. *Computational Linguistics*, 19(2):313–330.

Thomas Meyer and Andrei Popescu-Belis. 2012. Using Sense-labeled Discourse Connectives for Statistical Machine Translation. In *Proceedings of the EACL 2012 Joint Workshop on Exploiting Synergies between IR and MT, and Hybrid Approaches to MT (ESIRMT-HyTra)*, pages 129–138, Avignon, FR.

Lucie Mladová, Šárka Zikánová, Zuzanna Bedřichová, and Eva Hajičová. 2009. Towards a discourse corpus of Czech. In *Proceedings of the Corpus Linguistics Conference*, Liverpool, UK.

Franz Josef Och. 2003. Minimum Error Rate Training in Statistical Machine Translation. In *Proceedings of the 41st Annual Meeting of the Association for Computational Linguistics (ACL)*, pages 160–167, Sapporo, Japan.

Marie-Paule Péry-Woodley, Nicholas Asher, Patrice Enjalbert, Farah Benamara, Myriam Bras, Cécile Fabre, Stéphane Ferrari, Lydia-Mai Ho-Dac, Anne Le Draoulec, Yann Mathet, Philippe Muller, Laurent Prévot, Josette Rebeyrolle, Ludovic Tanguy, Marianne Vergez-Couret, Laure Vieu, and Antoine Widlöcher. 2009. ANNODIS: une approche outillée de l'annotation de structures discursives. In *Actes de la 16ème Conférence sur le Traitement Automatique des Langues Naturelles (TALN)*, Paris, France.

Andrei Popescu-Belis, Thomas Meyer, Jeevanthi Liyanapathirana, Bruno Cartoni, and Sandrine Zufferey. 2012. Discourse-level Annotation over Europarl for Machine Translation: Connectives and Pronouns. In *Proceedings of the eighth international conference on Language Resources and Evaluation (LREC)*, Istanbul, Turkey.

Rashmi Prasad, Nikhil Dinesh, Alan Lee, Eleni Miltsakaki, Livio Robaldo, Aravind Joshi, and Bonnie Webber. 2008. The Penn Discourse Treebank 2.0. In *Proceedings of 6th International Conference on Language Resources and Evaluation (LREC)*, pages 2961–2968, Marrakech, Morocco.

Manfred Stede. 2004. The Potsdam Commentary Corpus. In *Proceedings of the ACL Workshop on Discourse Annotation*, pages 96–102, Barcelona, Spain.

Andreas Stolcke, Jing Zheng, Wen Wang, and Victor Abrash. 2011. SRILM at Sixteen: Update and Outlook. In *Proceedings of the IEEE Automatic Speech Recognition and Understanding Workshop*, Waikoloa, Hawaii.

Yuping Zhou and Nianwen Xue. 2012. PDTB-style Discourse Annotation of Chinese Text. In *Proceedings of the 50th Annual Meeting on Association for Computational Linguistics (ACL)*, Jeju Island, Korea.

Translation of "It" in a Deep Syntax Framework

Michal Novák, Anna Nedoluzhko and **Zdeněk Žabokrtský**
Charles University in Prague, Faculty of Mathematics and Physics
Institute of Formal and Applied Linguistics
Malostranské náměstí 25, CZ-11800
{mnovak,nedoluzko,zabokrtsky}@ufal.mff.cuni.cz

Abstract

We present a novel approach to the translation of the English personal pronoun *it* to Czech. We conduct a linguistic analysis on how the distinct categories of *it* are usually mapped to their Czech counterparts. Armed with these observations, we design a discriminative translation model of *it*, which is then integrated into the TectoMT deep syntax MT framework. Features in the model take advantage of rich syntactic annotation TectoMT is based on, external tools for anaphoricity resolution, lexical co-occurrence frequencies measured on a large parallel corpus and gold coreference annotation. Even though the new model for *it* exhibits no improvement in terms of BLEU, manual evaluation shows that it outperforms the original solution in 8.5% sentences containing *it*.

1 Introduction

After it has long been neglected, retaining cohesion of a text larger than a single sentence in Machine Translation (MT) has recently become a discussed topic. Correct translation of referential expressions is in many cases essential for humans to grasp the meaning of a translated text.

Especially, the translation of pronouns attracts a higher rate of interest. In the previous works of Le Nagard and Koehn (2010), Hardmeier and Federico (2010) and Guillou (2012), it has been shown that current MT systems perform poorly in producing the correct forms of pronouns. As regards English, the personal pronoun *it* is the most complicated case. Not only can it corefer with almost any noun phrase (making it hard to pick the correct gender and number if the target language is morphologically rich), but it can also corefer with a larger discourse segment or play the role of a filler in certain grammatical constructions.

In this work, we turn our attention to the translation of the English personal pronoun *it* into Czech. Even if we ignore morphology and merge all related surface forms into one, we cannot find a single Czech expression that would comprise all functions of the English *it*. Moreover, there is no simple one-to-one mapping from categories of *it* to Czech expressions. For instance, one would expect that the translation of *it* which is coreferential with a noun phrase has to agree in number and gender with the translation of its antecedent. However, there are cases when it is more suitable to translate *it* as the demonstrative pronoun *to*, whose gender is always neuter.

The aim of this work is to build an English-to-Czech translation model for the personal pronoun *it* within the TectoMT framework (Žabokrtský et al., 2008). TectoMT is a tree-to-tree translation system with transfer via tectogrammatical layer, a deep syntactic layer which follows the Prague tectogrammatics theory (Sgall, 1967; Sgall et al., 1986) Therefore, its translation model outputs the deep syntactic representation of a Czech expression. Selecting the correct grammatical categories and thus producing a concrete surface form of a deep syntactic representation is provided by the translation synthesis stage, which we do not focus on in this work.

The mapping between *it* and corresponding Czech expressions depends on many aspects. We address them by introducing features based on syntactic annotation and anaphoricity resolver output. Furthermore, we make use of lexical co-occurrence counts aggregated on a large automatically annotated Czech-English parallel corpus CzEng 1.0 (Bojar et al., 2012). Coreference links also appear to be a source of valuable features.[1]

In contrast to the related work, we prefer a discriminative model to a commonly used generative

[1] However, we excluded them from the final model used in MT as they originate from gold standard annotation.

model. The former allows us to feed it with many syntactic and lexical features that may affect the output, which would hardly be possible in the latter.

2 Related Work

Our work addresses a similar issue that has been explored by Le Nagard and Koehn (2010), Hardmeier and Federico (2010) and Guillou (2012). These works attempted to incorporate information on coreference relations into MT, aiming to improve the translation of English pronouns into morphologically richer languages. The poor results in the first two works were mainly due to imperfect automatic coreference annotation.

The work of Guillou (2012) is of special interest to this work because it is also focused on English to Czech translation and makes an extensive use of the Prague Czech-English Dependency Treebank 2.0 (PCEDT). Instead of automatic coreference links, they employed gold annotation, revealing further reasons of small improvements – the number of occurrences in the tranining data weakened by including grammatical number and gender in the annotation and availability of only a single reference translation.

The first issue is a consequence of the assumption that a Czech pronoun must agree in gender and number with its antecedent. There are cases, though, when demonstrative pronoun *to* fits better and grammatical categories are not propagated. Keeping grammatical information on its antecedent may in this case result in probably not harmful but still superfluous partitioning the training data.

Our work deals also with the second issue, however, at the cost of partial manual annotating.

The most significant difference of our work compared to the abovementioned ones lies in the MT systems used. Whereas they tackle the issue of pronoun translation within the Moses phrase-based system (Koehn et al., 2003), we rely on the translation via deep syntax with TectoMT system (Žabokrtský et al., 2008). Our approach is more linguistically oriented, working with deep syntactic representations and postponing the decisions about the concrete forms to the synthesis stage.

3 Linguistic Analysis

In English, three main coarse-grained types of *it* are traditionally distinguished. Referential *it* points to a noun phrase in the preceding or the following context:

(1) Peter has finished writing an article and showed *it* to his supervisor.

Anaphoric *it* refers to a verbal phrase or larger discourse segments (so-called discourse deixis).

(2) Peter has discussed the issue with his supervisor and *it* helped him to finish the article.

Pleonastic *it* has no antecedent in the preceding/following context and its presence is imposed only by the syntactic rules of English.

(3) *It* is difficult to give a good example.

From the perspective of Czech, there are also three prevailing types of how *it* can be translated. The most frequent are personal pronouns or zero forms.[2] In Prague tectogrammatics theory zero anaphors are reconstructed on the tectogrammatical layer. Same as expressed personal pronouns, they are represented by a node with the *#PersPron* symbol, e.g.

(4) Bushova vláda oznámila, že se svůj plán *#PersPron* pokusí vzkřísit.

The Bush administration has said *it* will try to resurrect its plan.

The second typical possibility is the Czech demonstrative pronoun *to* (= it, this), which is a form of a pronoun *ten* in its neuter singular form, e.g.

(5) Analytik řekl, že *to* byla tato možnost požadavku, která pevnějším cenám pomohla.

The analyst said that *it* was the possibility of this demand that helped firm prices.

In many cases, it has no lexical counterpart in the Czech translation, the English and Czech sentences thus having a different syntactic structure. These are cases like, for instance:

(6) Obchodníci uvedli, že *je obtížné* nové emise REMIC strukturovat, když se ceny tolik mění.

Dealers noted that *it's difficult* to structure new Remics when prices are moving widely.

[2] Czech is a pro-drop language.

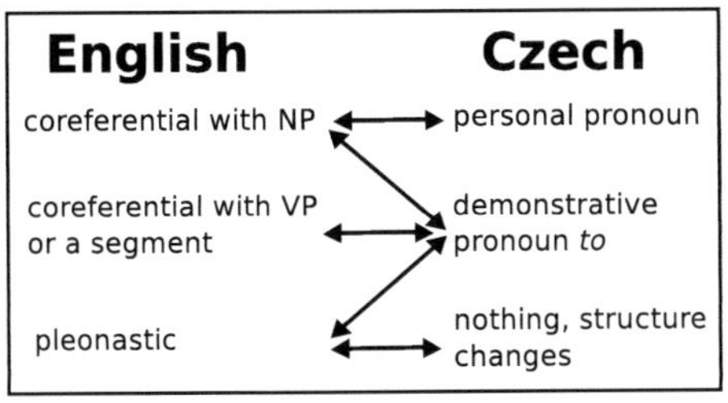

Figure 1: The mapping of the types of English *it* to Czech translations.

There are also some other possibilities of how *it* can be translated into Czech, such as the repetition of the antecedent noun, different genders of the demonstrative *ten* (=*it*, *this*) in the anaphoric position, using synonyms and hyperomyns. However, these cases are not so frequent and they rarely cannot be converted to one of the three broader categories.

The correspondence between the course-grained types of English *it* and its possible Czech translations is not one-to-one. As seen from Figure 1, a personal pronoun/zero anaphora translates to the referential *it* (see example 4) and no lexical counterpart is used when translating the pleonastic it (see example 6).

However, all types of *it* can be translated as a neuter demonstrative *to*. The typical case "*it* referring to VPs/larger discourse segments = *to*" was demonstrated in (5).

The mapping "referential *it* = *to*" is common for cases where the referent is attributed some further characteristics, mostly in constructions with a verb *to be* like "It is something.", such as (7).[3] This is an interesting case for Czech, because a gender and number agreement between the antecedent and the anaphoric *to* is generally absent.

(7) Some investors say Friday's sell-off was a good thing. "*It* was a healthy cleansing," says Michael Holland.

Někteří investoři říkají, že páteční výprodej byla dobrá věc. "Byla *to* zdravá očista," říká Michael Holland.

The "cleft sentences" (see example 8) and some other syntactic constructions are the case when pleonastic *it* is translated into Czech with the demonstrative *to*.

[3]We suspect that it holds also for *he/she/they* but such a claim is not yet empirically supported. For the sake of simplicity, we conduct our research only for *it*.

(8) But *it* is Mr. Lane, as movie director, who has been obsessed with refitting Chaplin's Little Tramp in a contemporary way.

Ale je *to* Lane jako filmový režisér, kdo je posedlý tím, že zmodernizuje Chaplinův film "Little Tramp (Malý tulák)".

In some cases, both translations of pleonastic *it* are possible: neuter demonstrative *to* or a different syntactic construction with no lexical counterpart of *it*. Compare the examples from PCEDT where *it* with similar syntactic function was translated by changing the syntactic structure in (9) and using a neuter *to* in (10):

(9) "*It was great* to have the luxury of time," Mr. Rawls said.

"*Bylo skvělé*, že jsme měli dostatek času," řekl Rawls.

(10) "On days that I'm really busy," says Ms. Foster, "*it seems decadent* to take time off for a massage."

"Ve dnech, kdy mám opravdu mnoho práce," říká paní Fosterová, "*to vypadá zvrhle*, když si vyhradím čas na masáž."

4 Translation via Deep Syntax

Following a phrase-based statistical MT approach, it may be demanding to tackle issues that arise when translating between typologically different languages. Translation from English to Czech is a typical example. One has to deal with a rich morphology, less constrained word order, changes in clauses bindings, pro-drops etc.

In this work, we make use of the English to Czech translation implemented within the TectoMT system, first introduced by Žabokrtský et al. (2008). In contrast to the phrase-based approach, TectoMT performs a tree-to-tree machine translation. Given an input English sentence, the translation process is divided into three stages: analysis, transfer and synthesis. TectoMT at first conducts an automatic analysis including POS tagging, named entity recognition, syntactic parsing, semantic role labeling, coreference resolution etc. This results in a deep syntactic representation of the English sentence, which is subsequently transferred into Czech, with the translation of lexical and grammatical information being provided via several factors. The process proceeds with a rule-based synthesis stage, when a surface Czech sentence is generated from its deep syntactic structure.

Deep syntactic representation of a sentence follows the Prague tectogrammatics theory (Sgall, 1967; Sgall et al., 1986). It is a dependency tree whose nodes correspond to the content words in the sentence. Personal pronouns missing on the surface are reconstructed in special nodes. Nodes are assigned semantic roles (called functors) and grammatical information is comprised in so called grammatemes. Furthermore, tectogrammatical representation is a place where coreference relations are annotated.

4.1 Model of *it* within TectoMT

The transfer stage, which maps an English tectogrammatical tree to a Czech one, is a place where the translation model of *it* is applied. For every English node corresponding to *it*, a feature vector is extracted and fed into a discriminative resolver that assigns one of the three classes to it – `PersPron`, `To` and `Null`, corresponding to the main Czech types introduced in Section 3.

If labeled as `PersPron`, the English node is mapped to a Czech *#PersPron* node and the English coreference link is projected. During the synthesis, it is decided whether the pronoun should be expressed on a surface, its gender and number are copied from the antecedent's head and finally the correct form (if any) is generated.

Obtaining class `To` makes things easier. The English node is only mapped to a Czech node containing the pronoun *ten* with its gender and number set to neuter singular, so that later the correct form *to* will be generated.

Last, if *it* is assigned `Null`, no corresponding node on the Czech side is generated, but the Czech counterpart of the governing verb is forced to be in neuter singular.

5 Prague Czech-English Dependency Treebank as a source of data

The Prague Czech-English Dependency Treebank (Hajič et al., 2011, PCEDT) is a manually parsed Czech-English parallel corpus comprising over 1.2 million words for each language in almost 50,000 sentence pairs. The English part contains the entire Penn Treebank–Wall Street Journal Section (Linguistic Data Consortium, 1999). The Czech part consists of translations of all the texts from the English part. The data from both parts are annotated on three layers following the theory of Prague tectogrammatics – the morphological layer (where each token from the sentence gets a lemma and a POS tag), the analytical layer (surface syntax in the form of a dependency tree, where each node corresponds to a token in the sentence) and the tectogrammatical representation (see Section 4).

Sentences of PCEDT have been automatically morphologically annotated and parsed into analytical dependency trees.[4] The tectogrammatical trees in both language parts have been annotated manually (Hajič et al., 2012). The nodes of Czech and English trees have been automatically aligned on analytical as well as tectogrammatical layer (Mareček et al., 2008).

5.1 Extraction of Classes

The shortcomings of the automatic alignment is particularly harmful for pronouns and zero anaphors, which can replace a whole range of content words and their meaning is inferred mainly from the context. The situation is better for verbs as their usual parents in dependency trees: since they carry meaning in a greater extent, their automatic alignment is of a higher quality.

Thus, we did not search for a Czech counterpart of *it* by following the alignment of *it* itself. Using the fact that the verb alignment is more reliable and functors in tectogrammatical trees have been manually corrected, we followed the alignment of the parent of *it* (a verb) and selected the Czech subtree with the same tectogrammatical functor as *it* had on the English side. If the obtained subtree is a single node of type *#PersPron* or *ten*, we assigned class `PersPron` or `To`, respectively, to the corresponding *it*. This approach relies also on the assumption that semantic roles do not change in the translation.

The automatic acquisition of classes covered more than 60% of instances, the rest had to be labeled manually. During the annotation, we obeyed the following rules:

1. If a demonstrative pronoun *to* is present in the Czech sentence or if a personal pronoun is either present or unexpressed, assign the instance to the corresponding class.

[4]The English dependency trees were built by automatically transforming the original phrase-structure annotation of the Penn Treebank.

2. Otherwise, ignore the Czech translation provided in the corpus and follow the most simplistic possible translation which would still be correct. Assign the instance to the class which fits it the best.

Note that it may happen that none of the three options fits, because it is either an idiomatic expression or larger structural modifications are required. Such cases are very rare and we left them out of the data.

The manual annotation was a bottleneck. We managed to tag the complete testing data, but were only able to annotate more than just 1/6 of the training data due to time reasons. We only use a corresponding proportion of the automatically labeled training instances in order to respect the overall distribution.

5.2 Extraction of Features

Given the linguistically supported observation on both manually and automatically annotated treebanks, we designed features to differentiate between the ways *it* is translated.

Since this work focuses on MT with transfer via deep-syntactic layer, it is possible for the proposed features to exploit morphological, syntactic and a little of semantic information present on various annotation layers.

Unlike the target classes, which have to be assigned as accurately as possible, extracted features must follow the real-world scenario of MT – the only information that is given is the source sentence. Thus, whereas extracting classes may exploit the gold standard linguistic annotation, it cannot be employed in feature extraction. We extract them from text automatically annotated by the same pipeline that is used in the TectoMT analysis stage.

However, there is an exception where we violate this approach – coreference. Performance of state-of-the-art coreference resolvers is still far from the ideal, especially for distinguishing between pronouns referring to noun phrases and those referring to clauses or wider discourse segments. Similarly to the work of Guillou (2012) we wanted to isolate the problem of translating referential expressions from the task of resolving the entity they refer to. Therefore, we opted for extracting the coreferential features from the gold annotation projected onto automatically analyzed trees. Note that the results achieved using these features have to be considered an upper bound for a given setting.

Although the mapping between Czech translation of *it* and English categories of *it* does not allow to translate *it* directly, the category of *it* estimated by an anaphoricity resolver might be a promising feature. We therefore constructed a binary feature based on the output of a system identifying whether a pronoun *it* is coreferential or not. We employed the NADA resolver (Bergsma and Yarowsky, 2011)[5] exploiting the web-scale n-gram data and its tree-based extension presented in (Veselovská et al., 2012).

Some verbs are more likely to bind with *it* that refers to a longer utterance. Such *it* is quite consistently translated as a demonstrative *to*. This motivated incorporating a parent lemma of an occurrence of *it* into the feature set. However, the training data is too small to be a sufficient sample from a distribution over lexical properties. Hence, we took advantage of the automatically annotated[6] Czech-English corpus CzEng 1.0 (Bojar et al., 2012) that comprises more than 15 million sentence pairs. In the manner described in Section 5.1, we collected co-occurrence counts between a functor that the given *it* possesses concatenated with a lemma of its verbal parent and a Czech counterpart having the same functor (denoted as $csit$). We filtered out all occurrences where $csit$ was neither *#PersPron* nor *ten*. Then, for both values of $csit$ a feature is constructed by looking up counts for a concrete occurrence in the collected counts and quantized into 4-5 bins (Bansal and Klein, 2012) following the formula:

$$bin(\log(\frac{count(functor : parent \wedge csit)}{count(functor : parent)count(csit)})).$$

Linguistic analysis carried out in Section 3 suggests the following syntax-oriented features related to the verb *to be*. Some nominal predicates tend to be translated as *to*, even though *it* is usually coreferential in such expressions (see example 7). So the corresponding binary feature fires if *it* is a subject and its parent is the verb *to be* having an object (Figure 2a).

Similarly, adjectival predicates that are not followed by a subordinating clause connected with

[5]A probability value returned by this tool was binarized at a threshold 0.5

[6]Using the same annotation layers as in PCEDT and TectoMT, i.e. in accordance with the Prague tectogrammatics theory.

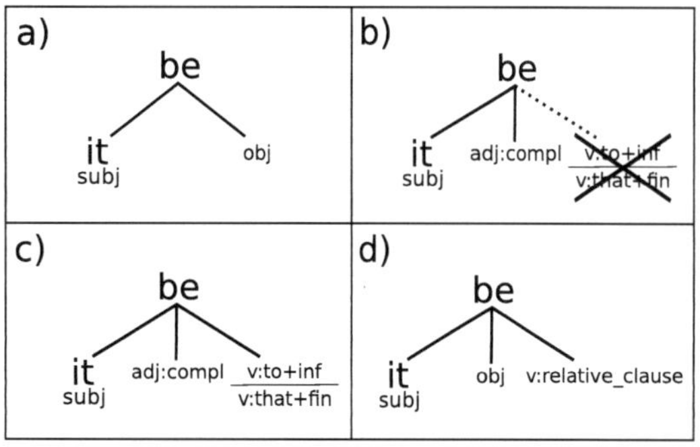

Figure 2: Syntactic features capturing typical constructions with a verb *be*.

the main clause by the English connectives *to* or *that* are usually referential and translated as *to*, too. We proposed a feature describing these cases, illustrated in Figure 2b.

In contrast, if an adjectival predicate is followed by a subordinating clause with the verb being finite and connected to the main clause by a conjunction *that*, in majority of cases it is a pleonastic usage of *it* translated as a null subject (see example 6). A schema of the feature is depicted in Figure 2c.

Being definitely pleonastic, *it* in cleft sentences is expressed in Czech either by *to* or by sentence rearranging (see example 8). We target this phenomenon by another feature being fired if *it* is a subject of the verb *to be* and if this verb has an object and is followed by a relative clause (see Figure 2d).

Finally, we designed two features exploiting coreference relations. The first one simply indicates if *it* has an antecedent, while the second fires if any of the antecedents in the coreferential chain is a verb phrase. As we noted above, these features are based on the gold standard annotation of coreference.

5.3 Data Description

The data for training and testing a discriminative translation model of the personal pronoun *it* were extracted from PCEDT with classes and features obtained as described in Section 5.1 and 5.2, respectively. Due to the limited amount of manually annotated training data, the training set extracted from sections 00 – 19 was reduced from 5841 to 940 instances, though. The testing set was annotated thoroughly, thus containing 543 instances extracted from sections 20 – 21. Every instance represents an occurrence of *it* in PCEDT. The distribution of target classes in the data is shown in Table 1.

Class	Train	Test
`PersPron`	576	322
`To`	231	138
`Null`	133	83

Table 1: Distribution of classes in the data sets.

6 Experiments

Experiments were conducted in two settings that differ in the usage of features extracted from gold coreferential relations.

To mitigate a possible error caused by a wrong classifier choice, we built several models based on various Machine Learning classification methods. If not explicitly mentioned, the methods below are applied with default parameters:

- **Vowpal Wabbit** (Langford, 2012). Binary logistic regression with one-against-all strategy for handling multiple classes. The optimum has been found using the online method (Stochastic Gradient Descent). We varied the parameters of the number of passes over the data and the L2 regularization weight.
- **AI::MaxEntropy**.[7] Multiclass logistic regression.[8] The optimum has been found using the batch method (L-BFGS).
- **sklearn.neighbors**.[9] `k`-nearest neighbors classifier with the parameter `k` being varied.
- **sklearn.tree**. Decision tree classifier.
- **sklearn.SVC**. Support Vector Machines with one-against-one strategy to handle multiple classes. We varied the choice of a kernel.

The accuracy evaluated on both training and test sets is shown in Table 2 (columns Acc:Train and Acc:Test). The baseline resolver simply picks the most frequent class in the training set, which is `PersPron`. For both experimental settings, the standard deviation measured on the test set is less than 1% in total, if the method's best configuration of parameters is taken and the result on decision trees, which we did not tune, is excluded. This shows that all classifiers are consistent in their decisions.

[7] `http://search.cpan.org/~laye/AI-MaxEntropy-0.20/`

[8] In the field of NLP also called Maximum Entropy.

[9] All classifiers labeled as sklearn.* are implemented in the Scikit-learn Python library (Pedregosa et al., 2011).

ML Method	all feats Acc:Train	Acc:Test	BLEU	all feats + coref Acc:Train	Acc:Test
Baseline	60.70	59.30	0.1401	60.70	59.30
Original TectoMT	–	–	**0.1404**	–	–
Vowpal Wabbit (passes=30)	90.62	75.69	–	90.83	75.87
Vowpal Wabbit (passes=20)	89.99	76.43	0.1403	90.20	76.98
Vowpal Wabbit (passes=10)	87.78	76.24	–	87.78	76.61
Vowpal Wabbit (passes=30, l2=0.001)	71.23	66.11	–	83.03	**77.16**
Vowpal Wabbit (passes=20, l2=0.001)	82.19	74.95	–	78.19	74.40
Vowpal Wabbit (passes=10, l2=0.001)	75.03	70.17	–	72.81	70.17
Vowpal Wabbit (passes=30, l2=0.00001)	90.52	75.69	–	90.94	76.06
Vowpal Wabbit (passes=20, l2=0.00001)	89.99	76.43	–	90.09	76.98
Vowpal Wabbit (passes=10, l2=0.00001)	87.67	76.24	–	87.67	76.61
AI::MaxEntropy	85.99	**76.61**	0.1403	86.09	76.98
sklearn.neighbors (k=1)	91.57	71.64	–	93.36	72.19
sklearn.neighbors (k=3)	84.62	72.01	–	84.93	71.82
sklearn.neighbors (k=5)	84.93	74.77	0.1403	84.72	75.87
sklearn.neighbors (k=10)	82.51	73.30	–	83.14	75.87
sklearn.tree	93.36	73.66	0.1403	94.10	71.82
sklearn.SVC (kernel=linear)	90.83	75.51	0.1402	91.15	76.80
sklearn.SVC (kernel=poly)	60.70	59.30	–	60.70	59.30
sklearn.SVC (kernel=rbf)	71.23	68.69	–	73.76	71.27

Table 2: Intrinsic (accuracy on the training and test data) and extrinsic (BLEU score) evaluation of translation model of *it* in configuration with (all feats) and without gold coreferential features (all feats + coref).

By introducing linguistically motivated features exploiting the deep-syntactic description of the sentence, we gained 17% in total over the baseline. Moreover, adding features based on the gold coreference annotation results in a further 0.5% improvement.

7 Evaluation on MT

Although intrinsic evaluation as performed in Section 6 can give us a picture of how accurate the translation model might be, the main purpose of this work is to integrate it in a full-fledged MT system. As explained in Section 4, this component is tailored for TectoMT – an MT system where the transfer is provided through a deep-syntactic layer.

The extrinsic evaluation of the proposed method was carried out on the English-Czech test set for WMT 2011 Shared Translation Task (Callison-Burch et al., 2011).[10] This data set contains 3,003 English sentences with one Czech reference translation, out of which 430 contain at least one occurrence of *it*.

Since this test set is provided with no annotation of coreferential links, the model of *it* that is involved in experiments on the end-to-end translation was trained on a complete feature set excluding the coreferential features using the Machine Learning method that performed best in the intrinsic test, i.e. AI::MaxEntropy (see Section 6).

The new method was compared to the rule-based approach originally used in TectoMT, which works as follows. In the transfer stage, all occurrences of *it* are translated to a demonstrative *ten*. In the synthesis stage, another rule is fired, which determines whether *ten* is omitted on the surface. Then, omitting it corresponds either to a structural change (`Null` class) or an unexpressed personal pronoun (a subset of `PersPron` class). It makes this original approach difficult to compare with the scores in Table 2, as the translation model of *it* is applied in the transfer stage, where we do not know yet if a personal pronoun is to be expressed or not. Thus, we consider it the most appropriate to use final translated sentences produced by two versions of TectoMT in order to compare the different way they handle *it*.

The shift from the original settings to a new model for *it* results in 166 changed sentences. In terms of BLEU score, we observe a marginal drop from 0.1404 to 0.1403 when using the new approach.[11] Other classifiers achieved the same or

[10] `http://www.statmt.org/wmt11/test.tgz`

[11] For comparison, the best system so far – Chimera (Bojar et al., 2013) achieves 0.1994 on the same test set. Chimera combines Moses, TectoMT and rule-based corrections.

new better than old	24
old better than new	13
both equally wrong	9
both equally correct	4

Table 3: The results of manual evaluation conducted on 50 sentences translated by TectoMT in the original settings (old) and with the new translation model for *it* (new)

similar score which correlates with the findings from intrinsic evaluation (see Table 2). It accords with a similar experience of Le Nagard and Koehn (2010) and Guillou (2012) and gives another evidence that the BLEU metric is inaccurate for measuring pronoun translation.

Manual evaluation gives a more realistic view. We randomly sampled 50 out of the 166 sentences that differ and one annotator assessed which of the two systems gave a better translation. Table 3 shows that in almost half of the cases the change was an improvement. Including the sentences that are acceptable for both settings, the new approach picked the correct Czech counterpart of *it* in 22% more sentences than the original approach. Since the proportion of the changed sentences accounts for almost 39% of all sentences containing *it*, the overall proportion of improved sentences with *it* is around 8.5% in total.

8 Discussion

Inspecting the manually evaluated translation for types of improvements and losses, we have found that in none of the changed sentences the original system decided to omit *ten* (obtained by the rule) on the surface. It shows that the new approach agrees with the original one on the way of omitting personal pronouns and mainly addresses the overly simplistic assignment of the demonstrative *ten*.

The distribution of target classes over corrected sentences is almost uniform. In 13 out of 24 improvements, the new system succeeded in correctly resolving the `Null` class while in the remaining 11 cases, the corrected class was `PersPron`. It took advantage mostly of the syntax-based features in the former and suggestions given by the NADA anaphoricity resolver in the latter.

Examining the errors, we observed that the majority of them are incurred in the structures with "it is". These errors stem mostly from incorrect activation of syntactic features due to parsing and POS tagging errors. Example 11 (the Czech sentence is an MT output) shows the latter, when the POS tagger erroneously labeled the word *soy* as an adjective. That resulted in activating the feature for adjectival predicates followed by *that* (Figure 2c) instead of a feature indicating cleft structures (Figure 2d), thus preferring the label `Null` to the correct `To`.

(11) SOURCE: *It is* just soy that all well-known manufacturers use now.

TECTOMT: *Je* ~~*to*~~ jen sójové, že známí výrobci všech používají teď.

9 Conclusion

In this work we presented a novel approach to dealing with the translation of the English personal pronoun *it*. We have shown that the mapping between the categories of *it* and the ways of translating it to Czech is not one-to-one. In order to deal with this, we designed a discriminative translation model of *it* for the TectoMT deep syntax MT framework.

We have built a system that outperforms its predecessor in 8.5% sentences containing *it*, taking advantage of the features based on rich syntactic annotation the MT system provides, external tools for anaphoricity resolution and features capturing lexical co-occurrence in a massive parallel corpus,

The main bottleneck that hampered bigger improvements is the manual annotation of the training data. We managed to accomplish it just on 1/6 of the data, which did not provide sufficient evidence for some specific features.

Our main objective of the future work is thus to reduce a need for manual annotation by discovering ways of automatic extraction of reliable classes from a semi-manually annotated corpus such as PCEDT.

Acknowledgments

This work has been supported by the Grant Agency of the Czech Republic (grants P406/12/0658 and P406/2010/0875), the grant GAUK 4226/2011 and EU FP7 project Khresmoi (contract no. 257528). This work has been using language resources developed and/or stored and/or distributed by the LINDAT-Clarin project of the Ministry of Education of the Czech Republic (project LM2010013).

References

Mohit Bansal and Dan Klein. 2012. Coreference Semantics from Web Features. In *Proceedings of the 50th Annual Meeting of the ACL: Long Papers – Volume 1*, pages 389–398, Stroudsburg, PA, USA. Association for Computational Linguistics.

Shane Bergsma and David Yarowsky. 2011. NADA: A Robust System for Non-Referential Pronoun Detection. In *DAARC*, pages 12–23, Faro, Portugal, October.

Ondřej Bojar, Zdeněk Žabokrtský, Ondřej Dušek, Petra Galuščáková, Martin Majliš, David Mareček, Jiří Maršík, Michal Novák, Martin Popel, and Aleš Tamchyna. 2012. The Joy of Parallelism with CzEng 1.0. In *Proceedings of LREC 2012*, Istanbul, Turkey, May. ELRA, European Language Resources Association.

Ondřej Bojar, Rudolf Rosa, and Aleš Tamchyna. 2013. Chimera – Three Heads for English-to-Czech Translation. In *Proceedings of the Eight Workshop on Statistical Machine Translation*. Under review.

Chris Callison-Burch, Philipp Koehn, Christof Monz, and Omar Zaidan. 2011. Findings of the 2011 Workshop on Statistical Machine Translation. In *Proceedings of the Sixth Workshop on Statistical Machine Translation*, pages 22–64, Edinburgh, Scotland, July. Association for Computational Linguistics.

Liane Guillou. 2012. Improving Pronoun Translation for Statistical Machine Translation. In *Proceedings of the Student Research Workshop at the 13th Conference of the EACL*, pages 1–10, Stroudsburg, PA, USA. Association for Computational Linguistics.

Jan Hajič, Eva Hajičová, Jarmila Panevová, Petr Sgall, Silvie Cinková, Eva Fučíková, Marie Mikulová, Petr Pajas, Jan Popelka, Jiří Semecký, Jana Šindlerová, Jan Štěpánek, Josef Toman, Zdeňka Urešová, and Zdeněk Žabokrtský. 2011. Prague Czech-English Dependency Treebank 2.0.

Jan Hajič, Eva Hajičová, Jarmila Panevová, Petr Sgall, Ondřej Bojar, Silvie Cinková, Eva Fučíková, Marie Mikulová, Petr Pajas, Jan Popelka, Jiří Semecký, Jana Šindlerová, Jan Štěpánek, Josef Toman, Zdeňka Urešová, and Zdeněk Žabokrtský. 2012. Announcing Prague Czech-English Dependency Treebank 2.0. In *Proceedings of the 8th International Conference on Language Resources and Evaluation (LREC 2012)*, pages 3153–3160. ELRA.

Christian Hardmeier and Marcello Federico. 2010. Modelling Pronominal Anaphora in Statistical Machine Translation. In Marcello Federico, Ian Lane, Michael Paul, and François Yvon, editors, *Proceedings of the seventh International Workshop on Spoken Language Translation (IWSLT)*, pages 283–289.

Philipp Koehn, Franz Josef Och, and Daniel Marcu. 2003. Statistical Phrase-based Translation. In *Proceedings of the 2003 Conference of the NAACL HLT – Volume 1*, pages 48–54, Stroudsburg, PA, USA. Association for Computational Linguistics.

John Langford. 2012. Vowpal Wabbit.

Ronan Le Nagard and Philipp Koehn. 2010. Aiding Pronoun Translation with Co-Reference Resolution. In *Proceedings of the Joint Fifth Workshop on Statistical Machine Translation and MetricsMATR*, pages 252–261, Uppsala, Sweden, July. Association for Computational Linguistics.

Linguistic Data Consortium. 1999. Penn Treebank 3. LDC99T42.

David Mareček, Zdeněk Žabokrtský, and Václav Novák. 2008. Automatic Alignment of Czech and English Deep Syntactic Dependency Trees. In *Proceedings of the Twelfth EAMT Conference*, pages 102–111.

Fabian Pedregosa, Gaël Varoquaux, Alexandre Gramfort, Vincent Michel, Bertrand Thirion, Olivier Grisel, Mathieu Blondel, Peter Prettenhofer, Ron Weiss, Vincent Dubourg, Jake Vanderplas, Alexandre Passos, David Cournapeau, Matthieu Brucher, Matthieu Perrot, and Édouard Duchesnay. 2011. Scikit-learn: Machine Learning in Python. *Journal of Machine Learning Research*, 12:2825–2830, November.

Petr Sgall, Eva Hajičová, and Jarmila Panevová. 1986. *The Meaning of the Sentence in Its Semantic and Pragmatic Aspects*. D. Reidel Publishing Company, Dordrecht.

Petr Sgall. 1967. *Generativní popis jazyka a česká deklinace*. Academia, Prague, Czech Republic.

Kateřina Veselovská, Giang Linh Nguy, and Michal Novák. 2012. Using Czech-English Parallel Corpora in Automatic Identification of It. In *The Fifth Workshop on Building and Using Comparable Corpora*, pages 112–120.

Zdeněk Žabokrtský, Jan Ptáček, and Petr Pajas. 2008. TectoMT: Highly Modular MT System with Tectogrammatics Used as Transfer Layer. In *Proceedings of the Third Workshop on Statistical Machine Translation*, pages 167–170, Stroudsburg, PA, USA. Association for Computational Linguistics.

Feature Weight Optimization for Discourse-Level SMT

Sara Stymne, Christian Hardmeier, Jörg Tiedemann and Joakim Nivre
Uppsala University
Department of Linguistics and Philology
Box 635, 751 26 Uppsala, Sweden
firstname.lastname@lingfil.uu.se

Abstract

We present an approach to feature weight optimization for document-level decoding. This is an essential task for enabling future development of discourse-level statistical machine translation, as it allows easy integration of discourse features in the decoding process. We extend the framework of sentence-level feature weight optimization to the document-level. We show experimentally that we can get competitive and relatively stable results when using a standard set of features, and that this framework also allows us to optimize document-level features, which can be used to model discourse phenomena.

1 Introduction

Discourse has largely been ignored in traditional machine translation (MT). Typically each sentence has been translated in isolation, essentially yielding translations that are bags of sentences. It is well known from translation studies, however, that discourse is important in order to achieve good translations of documents (Hatim and Mason, 1990). Most attempts to address discourse-level issues for statistical machine translation (SMT) have had to resort to solutions such as post-processing to address lexical cohesion (Carpuat, 2009) or two-step translation to address pronoun anaphora (Le Nagard and Koehn, 2010). Recently, however, we presented Docent (Hardmeier et al., 2012; Hardmeier et al., 2013), a decoder based on local search that translates full documents. So far this decoder has not included a feature weight optimization framework. However, feature weight optimization, or tuning, is important for any modern SMT decoder to achieve a good translation performance.

In previous research with Docent, we used grid search to find weights for document-level features while base features were optimized using standard sentence-level techniques. This approach is impractical since many values for the extra features have to be tried, and, more importantly, it might not give the same level of performance as jointly optimizing all parameters. Principled feature weight optimization is thus essential for researchers that want to use document-level features to model discourse phenomena such as anaphora, discourse connectives, and lexical consistency. In this paper, we therefore propose an approach that supports discourse-wide features in document-level decoding by adapting existing frameworks for sentence-level optimization. Furthermore, we include a thorough empirical investigation of this approach.

2 Discourse-Level SMT

Traditional SMT systems translate texts sentence by sentence, assuming independence between sentences. This assumption allows efficient algorithms based on dynamic programming for exploring a large search space (Och et al., 2001). Because of the dynamic programming assumptions it is hard to directly include discourse-level features into a traditional SMT decoder. Nevertheless, there have been several attempts to integrate intersentential and long distance models for discourse-level phenomena into standard decoders, usually as ad-hoc additions to standard models, addressing a single phenomenon.

Several studies have tried to improve pronoun anaphora by adding information about the antecedent, either by using two-step decoding (Le Nagard and Koehn, 2010; Guillou, 2012) or by extracting information from previously translated sentences (Hardmeier and Federico, 2010), unfortunately without any convincing results. To address the translation of discourse connectives, source-side pre-processing has been used to annotate surface forms either in the corpus or in the phrase-table (Meyer and Popescu-Belis, 2012) or by using factored decoding (Meyer et al., 2012) to disambiguate connectives, with small improvements. Lexical consistency has been addressed by the use of post-processing (Carpuat, 2009), multi-pass decoding (Xiao et al., 2011; Ture et al., 2012), and cache models (Tiedemann, 2010; Gong et al., 2011). Gong et al. (2012) addressed the issue of tense selection for translation from Chinese, by the use of inter-sentential tense n-grams, exploiting information from previously translated sentences. Another way to use a larger context is by integrating word sense disambiguation and SMT. This has been done by re-initializing phrase probabilities for each sentence (Carpuat and Wu, 2007), by introducing extra features in the phrase-table (Chan et al., 2007), or as a k-best re-ranking task (Specia et al., 2008). Another type of approach is to integrate topic modeling into phrase tables (Zhao and Xing, 2010; Su et al., 2012). For a more thorough overview of discourse in SMT, see Hardmeier (2012).

Here we instead choose to work with the recent document-level SMT decoder Docent (Hardmeier et al., 2012). Unlike in traditional decoding were documents are generated sentence by sentence, feature models in Docent always have access to the complete discourse context, even before decoding is finished. It implements the phrase-based SMT approach (Koehn et al., 2003) and is based on local search, where a state consists of a full translation of a document, which is improved by applying a series of operations to improve the translation. A hill-climbing strategy is used to find a (local) maximum. The operations allow changing the translation of a phrase, changing the word order by swapping the positions of two phrases, and resegmenting phrases. The initial state can either be initialized randomly in monotonic order, or be based on an initial run from a standard sentence-based decoder. The number of iterations in the decoder is controlled by two parameters, the maximum number of iterations and a rejection limit, which stops the decoder if no change was made in a certain number of iterations. This setup is not limited by dynamic programming constraints, and enables the use of the translated target document to extract features. It is thus easy to directly integrate discourse-level features into Docent. While we use this specific decoder in our experiments, the method proposed for document-level feature weight optimization is not limited to it. It can be used with any decoder that outputs feature values at the document level.

3 Sentence-Level Tuning

Traditionally, feature weight optimization, or tuning, for SMT is performed by an iterative process where a development set is translated to produce a k-best list. The parameters are then optimized using some procedure, generally to favor translations in the k-best list that have a high score on some MT metric. The translation step is then repeated using the new weights for decoding, and optimization is continued on a new k-best list, or on a combination of all k-best lists. This is repeated until some end condition is satisfied, for instance for a set number of iterations, until there is only very small changes in parameter weights, or until there are no new translations in the k-best lists.

SMT tuning is a hard problem in general, partly because the correct output is unreachable and also because the translation process includes latent variables, which means that many efficient standard optimization procedures cannot be used (Gimpel and Smith, 2012). Nevertheless, there are a number of techniques including MERT (Och, 2003), MIRA (Chiang et al., 2008; Cherry and Foster, 2012), PRO (Hopkins and May, 2011), and Rampion (Gimpel and Smith, 2012). All of these optimization methods can be plugged into the standard optimization loop. All of the methods work relatively well in practice, even though there are limitations, for instance that many methods are non-deterministic meaning that their results are somewhat unstable. However, there are some important differences. MERT is based on scores for the full test set, whereas the other methods are based on sentence-level scores. MERT also has the drawback that it only works well for small sets of features. In this paper we are not concerned with the actual optimization algorithm and its properties, though, but instead we focus on the integration of document-level decoding into the existing optimization frameworks.

In order to adapt sentence-level frameworks to our needs we need to address the granularity of scoring and the process of extracting k-best lists. For document-level features we do not have meaningful scores on the sentence level which are required in standard optimization frameworks. Furthermore, the extraction of k-best lists is not as

Input: inputDocs, refDocs, init weights θ_0, max decoder iters max, sample start ss, sample interval si,
Output: learned weights θ

```
θ ← θ0
Initialize empty klist
run ← 1
repeat
    Initialize empty klist_run
    for doc ← 1, inputDocs.size do Initialize decoder state randomly for inputDocs[doc]
        for iter ← 1, max do
            Perform one hill-climbing step for inputDocs[doc]
            if iter >= ss & iter mod si == 0 then
                Add translation for inputDocs[doc] to klist_run
            end if
        end for
    end for
    Merge klist_run with klist
    modelScores_doc ← ComputeModelScores(klist)
    metricStats_doc ← ComputeMetricStats(klist, refDocs)
    θ_run ← θ
    θ ← Optimize(θ_run, modelScores_doc, metricStats_doc)
    run ← run + 1
until Done(run, θ, θ_run)
```

Figure 1: Document-level feature weight optimization algorithm

straightforward in our hill-climbing decoder as in standard sentence-level decoders such as Moses (Koehn et al., 2007) where such a list can be approximated easily from the internal beam search strategy. Working on output lattices is another option in standard approaches (Cherry and Foster, 2012) which is also not applicable in our case.

In the following section we describe how we can address these issues in order to adapt sentence-level frameworks for our purposes.

4 Document-Level Tuning

To allow document-level feature weight optimization, we make some small changes to the sentence-level framework. Figure 1 shows the algorithm we use. It assumes access to an optimization algorithm, `Optimize`, and an end criterion, `Done`. The changes from standard sentence-level optimization is that we compute scores on the document level, and that we sample translations instead of using standard k-best lists.

The main challenge is that we need meaningful scores which we do not have at the sentence level in document decoding. We handle this by simply computing all scores (model scores and metric scores) exclusively at the document level. Remember that all standard MT metrics based on sentence-level comparisons with reference translations can be aggregated for a complete test set. Here we do the same for all sentences in a given document. This can actually be an advantage compared to optimization methods that use sentence-level scores, which are known to be unreliable (Callison-Burch et al., 2012). Document-level scores should thus be more stable, since they are based on more data. A potential drawback is that we get fewer data points with a test set of the same size, which might mean that we need more data to achieve as good results as with sentence-level optimization. We will see the ability of our approach to optimize weights with reasonable data sets in our experiments further down.

The second problem, the extraction of k-best lists can be addressed in several ways. It is possible to get a k-best list from Docent by extracting the results from the last k iterations. However, since Docent operates on the document-level and does not accept updates in each iteration, there will be many identical and/or very similar hypotheses with such an approach. Another option would be to extract the translations from the k last different iterations, which would require some small changes to the decoder. Instead, we opt to use k-lists, lists of translations sampled with some interval, which contains k translations, but not necessarily all the k best translations that could be found by the decoder. A k-best list is of course a k-list, which we get with a sample interval of 1.

We also choose to restart Docent randomly in each optimization iteration, since it allows us to explore a larger part of the search space. We empirically found that this strategy worked better than restarting the decoder from the previous best state.

	German–English			English–Swedish		
	Type	Sentences	Documents	Type	Sentences	Documents
Training	Europarl	1.9M	–	Europarl	1.5M	–
	News Commentary	178K	–	–	–	–
Tuning	News2009	2525	111	Europarl (Moses)	2000	–
	News2008-2010	7567	345	Europarl (Docent)	1338	100
Test	News2012	3003	99	Europarl	690	20

Table 1: Domain and number of sentences and documents for the corpora

As seen in Figure 1, there are some additional parameters in our procedure: the sample start iteration and the sample interval. We also need to set the number of decoder iterations to run. In Section 5 we empirically investigate the effect of these parameters.

Compared to sentence-level optimization, we also have a smaller number of units to get scores from, since we use documents as units, and not sentences. The importance of this depends on the optimization algorithm. MERT calculates metric scores over the full tuning set, not for individual sentences, and should not be affected too much by the change in granularity. Many other optimization algorithms, like PRO, work on the sentence level, and will likely be more affected by the reduction of units. In this work we focus on MERT, which is the most commonly used optimization procedure in the SMT community, and which tends to work quite well with relatively few features. However, we also show contrastive results for PRO (Hopkins and May, 2011). A further issue is that Docent is non-deterministic, i.e., it can give different results with the same parameter weights. Since the optimization process is already somewhat unstable this is a potential issue that needs to be explored further, which we do in Section 5.

Implementation-wise we adapted Docent to output k-lists and adapted the infrastructure available for tuning in the Moses decoder (Koehn et al., 2007) to work with document-level scores. This setup allows us to use the variety of optimization procedures implemented there.

5 Experiments

In this section we report experimental results where we investigate several issues in connection with document-level feature weight optimization for SMT. We first describe the experimental setup, followed by baseline results using sentence-level optimization. We then present validation experiments with standard sentence-level features, which can be compared to standard optimization. Finally, we report results with a set of document-level features that have been proposed for joint translation and text simplification (Stymne et al., 2013).

5.1 Experimental Setup

Most of our experiments are for German-to-English news translation using data from the WMT13 workshop.[1] We also show results with document-level features for English-to-Swedish Europarl (Koehn, 2005). The size of the training, tuning, and test sets are shown in Table 1. First of all, we need to extract documents for tuning and testing with Docent. Fortunately, the news data already contain document markup, corresponding to individual news articles. For Europarl we define a document as a consecutive sequence of utterances from a single speaker. To investigate the effect of the size of the tuning set, we used different subsets of the available tuning data.

All our document-level experiments are carried out with Docent but we also contrast with the Moses decoder (Koehn et al., 2007). For the purpose of comparison, we use a standard set of sentence-level features used in Moses in most of our experiments: five translation model features, one language model feature, a distance-based reordering penalty, and a word count feature. For feature weight optimization we also apply the standard settings in the Moses toolkit. We optimize towards the Bleu metric, and optimization ends either when no weights are changed by more than 0.00001, or after 25 iterations. MERT is used unless otherwise noted.

Except for one of our baselines, we always run Docent with random initialization. For test we run the document decoder for a maximum of 2^{27} iterations with a rejection limit of 100,000. In our experiments, the decoder always stopped when reaching the rejection limit, usually between 1–5

[1] http://www.statmt.org/wmt13/translation-task.html

million iterations.

We show results on the Bleu (Papineni et al., 2002) and NIST (Doddington, 2002) metrics. For German–English we show the average result and standard deviation of three optimization runs, to control for optimizer instability as proposed by Clark et al. (2011). For English–Swedish we report results on single optimization runs, due to time constraints.

5.2 Baselines

Most importantly, we would like to show the effectiveness of the document-level tuning procedure described above. In order to do this, we created a baseline using sentence-level optimization with a tuning set of 2525 sentences and the News2009 corpus for evaluation. Increasing the tuning set is known to give only modest improvements (Turchi et al., 2012; Koehn and Haddow, 2012).

The feature weights optimized with the standard Moses decoder can then directly be used in our document-level decoder as we only include sentence-level features in our baseline model. As expected, these optimized weights also lead to a better performance in document-level decoding compared to an untuned model as shown in Table 2. Note, that Docent can be initialized in two ways, by Moses and randomly. Not surprisingly, the result for the runs initialized with Moses are identical with the pure sentence-level decoder. Initializing randomly gives a slightly lower Bleu score but with a larger variation than with Moses initialization, which is also expected. Docent is non-deterministic, and can give somewhat varying results with the same weights. However, this variation has been shown experimentally to be very small (Hardmeier et al., 2012).

Our goal now is to show that document-level tuning can perform equally well in order to verify our approach. For this, we set up a series of experiments looking at varying tuning sets and different parameters of the decoding and optimization procedure. With this we like to demonstrate the stability of the document-level feature weight optimization approach presented above. Note that the most important baselines for comparison with the results in the next sections are the ones with Docent and random initialization.

5.3 Sentence-Level Features

In this section we present validation results where we investigate different aspects of document-level feature weight optimization with standard sentence-level features. In this way we can compare the results directly to standard sentence-level optimization, and to the results of Moses.

System	Tuning	Bleu	NIST
Moses	None	17.7	6.25
Docent-M	None	17.7	6.25
Docent-R	None	15.2 (0.05)	5.88 (0.00)
Moses	Moses	18.3 (0.04)	6.22 (0.01)
Docent-M	Moses	18.3 (0.04)	6.22 (0.01)
Docent-R	Moses	18.1 (0.13)	6.23 (0.01)

Table 2: Baseline results, where Docent-M is initialized with Moses and Docent-R randomly

Docs	Sent.	Min	Max	Bleu	NIST
111	2525	3	127	18.0 (0.11)	6.19 (0.04)
345	7567	3	127	18.1 (0.14)	6.25 (0.02)
100	1921	8	40	18.0 (0.05)	6.25 (0.10)
200	3990	8	40	17.9 (0.25)	6.20 (0.09)
100	2394	8	100	18.0 (0.12)	6.27 (0.07)
200	4600	8	100	18.1 (0.29)	6.26 (0.10)
300	6852	8	100	18.2 (0.13)	6.27 (0.03)

Table 3: Results for German–English with varying sizes of tuning set, where the number of sentences and documents are varied, as well as the minimum and maximum number of sentences per document

Corpus size We investigate how tuning is affected by corpus size. The corpus size was varied in two ways, by changing the number of documents in the tuning set, and by changing the length of documents in the tuning sets. In this experiment we run 20000 decoder iterations per optimization iteration, and use a k-list of size 101, with sample interval 100. Table 3 shows the results with varying tuning set sizes for German–English. There is very little variation between the scores, and no clear tendencies. All results are of similar quality to the baseline with random initialization and sentence-level tuning, and better than not using any tuning. The top line in Table 3 is News2009, the same tuning set as for the baselines. The scores are somewhat more unstable than the baseline scores, but stability is not related to corpus size. In the following sections we will use the tuning set with 200 documents, size 8-40.

Number of decoder iterations and k-list sampling Two issues that are relevant for feature weight optimization with the document-level decoder is the number of decoder hill-climbing iterations in each optimization iteration, and the settings for k-list sampling. These choices affect the

Iterations	K-list	UTK	Bleu	NIST
20000	101	55.6	17.9 (0.25)	6.20 (0.09)
30000	201	67.2	17.9 (0.06)	6.21 (0.01)
40000	301	79.9	18.2 (0.11)	6.28 (0.09)
50000	401	86.9	18.1 (0.20)	6.22 (0.05)
75000	651	99.2	17.8 (0.15)	6.13 (0.03)
100000	901	106.8	17.9 (0.17)	6.16 (0.03)
30000	101	21.6	18.0 (0.15)	6.21 (0.02)
40000	101	12.6	17.7 (0.53)	6.12 (0.15)
50000	101	8.2	17.9 (0.24)	6.18 (0.06)

Table 4: Results for German–English with a varying number of iterations and k-list size (UTK is the average number of unique translations per document in the k-lists)

Interval	Start	UTK	Bleu	NIST
1	19900	1.4	18.2 (0.07)	6.25 (0.04)
10	19000	5.2	18.1 (0.08)	6.22 (0.03)
100	10000	55.6	17.9 (0.25)	6.20 (0.09)
200	0	82.2	17.9 (0.19)	6.15 (0.05)

Table 5: Results with different k-list-sample intervals for k-lists size 101 (UTK is the average number of unique translations per document in the k-lists)

quality of the translations in each optimization iteration, and the spread in the k-list. We will report the average number of unique translations per document in the k-lists, *UTK*, during feature weight optimization, in this section.

The top half of Table 4 shows results with a different number of iterations, when we sample k-lists from iteration 10000 with interval 100 for German–English, which means that the size of the k-lists also changes. The differences on MT metrics are very small. The number of new unique translations in the k-lists decrease with the number of decoder iterations. With 20K iterations, 55% of the k-lists entries are unique, which could be compared to only 12% with 100K iterations. The majority of the unique translations are thus found in the beginning of the decoding, which is not surprising.

The bottom half of Table 4 shows results with a different number of decoder iterations, but a set k-list size. In this setting the number of unique hypotheses in the k-lists obviously decreases with the number of decoder iterations. Despite this, there are mostly small result differences, except for 40K iterations, which has more unstable results than the other settings. It does not seem useful to increase the number of decoder iterations without also increasing the size of the k-list. An even better strategy might be to only include unique entries in the k-lists. We will explore this in future work.

We also ran experiments where we did not restart the decoder with a random state in each iteration, but instead saved the previous state and continued decoding with the new weights from there. This, however, was largely unsuccessful, and gave very low scores. We believe that the reason for this is mainly that a much smaller part of the search space is explored when the decoder is not restarted with a new seed repeatedly. The fact that a higher overall quality can be achieved with a higher number of iterations (see Figure 2) can apparently not compensate for this drawback.

Finally, we investigate the effect of the sample interval for the k-lists. To get k-lists of equal size, 101, we start the sampling at different iterations. Table 5 shows the results, and we can see that with a small sample interval, the number of unique translations decreases drastically. Despite this, there are no large result differences. There is actually a slight trend that a smaller sample interval is better. This does not confirm our intuition that it is important with many different translations in the k-list. Especially for interval 1 it is surprising, since there is often only 1 unique translation for a single document. We believe that the fact that k-lists from different iterations are joined, can be part of the explanation for these results. We think more work is needed in the future, to further explore these settings, and the interaction with the total number of decoder iteration, and the k-list sampling.

To further shed some light to these results, we show learning curves from the optimization. Figure 2 shows Bleu scores for the system optimized with 100K decoder iterations after different numbers of iterations, for the last three iterations in each of the three optimization runs. As shown in Hardmeier et al. (2012), the translation quality increases fast at first, but start to level out at around 40K iterations. Despite this, the optimization results are good even with 20K iterations, which is somewhat surprising. Figures 3 and 4 show the Bleu scores after each tuning iteration for the systems in Tables 4 and 5. As is normal for SMT tuning, the convergence is slow, and there are some oscillations even late in the optimization. Overall systems with many iterations seem somewhat more stable.

Overall, the results are better than the untuned

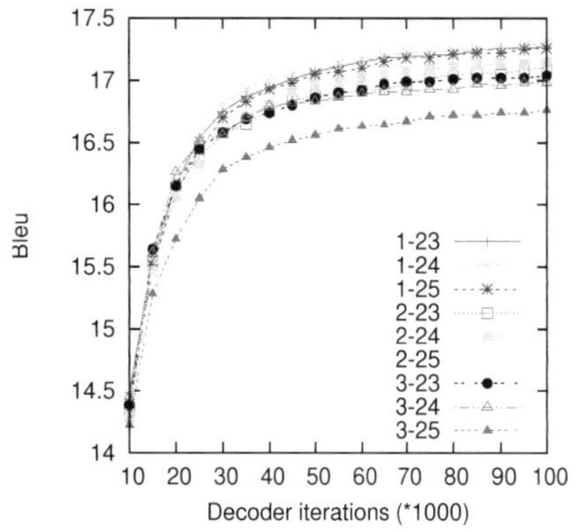

Figure 2: Bleu scores during 100000 Docent iterations during feature weight optimization

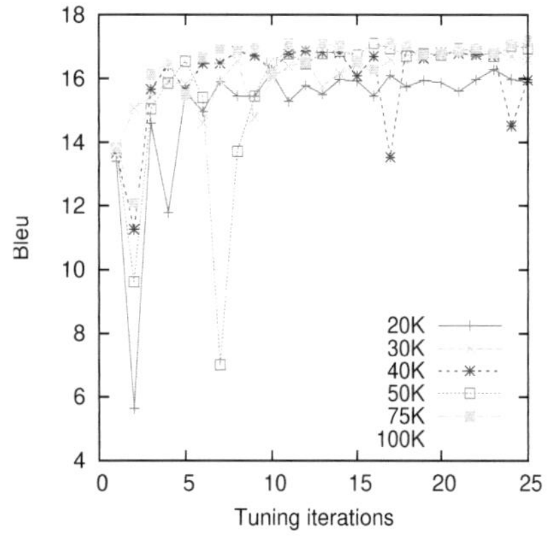

Figure 3: Bleu scores during feature weight optimization for systems with different number of decoder iterations and k-list sizes.

baseline and on par with the sentence-level tuning baselines in all settings, with a relatively modest variation, even across settings. In fact, if we calculate the total scores of all 36 systems in Tables 4 and 5, we get a Bleu score of 18.0 (0.23) and a NIST score of 6.19 (0.07), with a variation that is not higher than for many of the different settings.

Optimization method In this section we compare the performance of the MERT optimization algorithm with that of PRO, and a combination that starts MERT with weights initialized with PRO (MERT+PRO), suggested by Koehn and Haddow (2012). Here we run 30000 decoder iterations. Table 6 shows the results. Initializing MERT with PRO did not affect the scores much. The scores with only PRO, however, are slightly lower than for MERT, and have a much larger score variation. This could be because PRO is

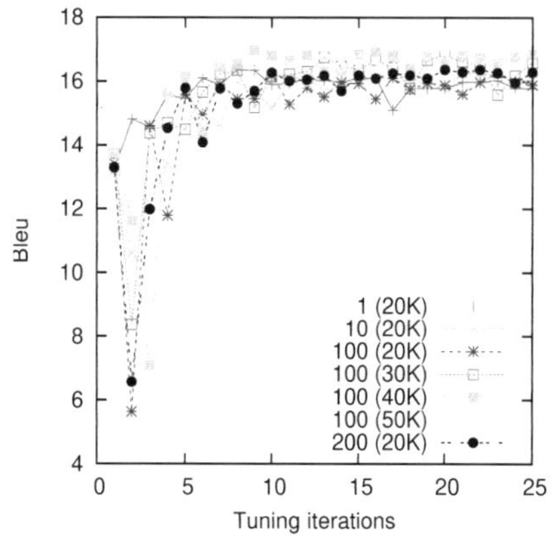

Figure 4: Bleu scores during feature weight optimization for systems with different k-list sample interval and number of decoder iterations.

	Bleu	NIST
MERT	17.9 (0.06)	6.21 (0.01)
PRO	17.5 (0.41)	6.15 (0.20)
MERT+PRO	18.0 (0.12)	6.18 (0.06)

Table 6: Results with different optimization algorithms for German–English

likely to need more data, since it calculates metric scores on individual units, sentences or documents, not across the full tuning set, like MERT. This likely means that 200 documents are too few for stable results with optimization methods that depend on unit-level metric scores.

5.4 Document-Level Features

In this section we investigate the effect of optimization with a number of document-level features. We use a set of features proposed in Stymne et al. (2013), in order to promote the readability of texts. In this scenario, however, we use these features in a standard SMT setting, where they can potentially improve the lexical consistency of translations. The features are:

- Type token ratio (TTR) – the ratio of types, unique words, to tokens, total number of words
- OVIX – a reformulation of TTR that has traditionally been used for Swedish and that is less sensible to text length than TTR, see Eq. 1
- Q-value, phrase level (QP) - The Q-value was developed as a measure for bilingual term quality (Deléger et al., 2006), to promote common and consistently translated terms. See Eq. 2, where $f(st)$ is the frequency of

System	Optimization	German–English Bleu	German–English NIST	English–Swedish Bleu	English–Swedish NIST
Moses	Sentence	18.3 (0.04)	6.22 (0.01)	24.3	6.12
Docent	Sentence	18.1 (0.13)	6.23 (0.01)	24.1	6.06
Docent	Document	17.9 (0.25)	6.20 (0.09)	23.4	6.01
TTR	Document	18.3 (0.16)	6.33 (0.04)	23.6	6.15
OVIX	Document	18.3 (0.13)	6.30 (0.03)	23.4	5.99
QW	Document	18.1 (0.14)	6.22 (0.03)	24.2	6.11
QP	Document	18.0 (0.10)	6.23 (0.05)	21.2	5.70

Table 7: Results when using document-level features

the phrase pair, $n(s)$ is the number of unique target phrases which the source phrase is aligned to in the document, and $n(t)$ is the same for the target phrase. Here the Q-value is applied on the phrase level.

- Q-value, word level (QW) - Same as above, but here we apply the Q-value for source words and their alignments on the target side.

$$\text{OVIX} = \frac{\log(\text{count}(\text{tokens}))}{\log\left(2 - \frac{\log(\text{count}(\text{types}))}{\log(\text{count}(\text{tokens}))}\right)} \quad (1)$$

$$\text{Q-value} = \frac{f(st)}{n(s) + n(t)} \quad (2)$$

We added these features one at a time to the standard feature set. Optimization was performed with 20000 decoder iterations, and a k-list of size 101. As shown in the previous sections, there are slightly better settings, which could have been used to boost the results somewhat.

The results are shown in Table 7. For German–English, the results are generally on par with the baselines for Bleu and slightly higher on NIST for OVIX and TTR. For English–Swedish, we used a smaller tuning set on the document level than on the sentence level, see Table 1, due to time constraints. This is reflected in the scores, which are generally lower than for sentence-level decoding. Using the QW feature, however, we receive competitive scores to the sentence-based baselines, which indicates that it can be meaningful to use document-level features with the suggested tuning approach.

While the results do not improve much over the baselines, these experiments still show that we can optimize discourse-level features with our approach. We need to identify more useful document-level features in future work, however.

6 Conclusion

We have shown how the standard feature weight optimization workflow for SMT can be adapted to document-level decoding, which allows easy integration of discourse-level features into SMT. We modified the standard framework by calculating scores on the document-level instead of the sentence level, and by using k-lists rather than k-best lists.

Experimental results show that we can achieve relatively stable results, on par with the results for sentence-level optimization and better than without tuning, with standard features. This is despite the fact that we use the hill-climbing decoder without initialization by a standard decoder, which means that it is somewhat unstable, and is not guaranteed to find any global maximum, even according to the model. We also show that we can optimize document-level features successfully. We investigated the effect of a number of parameters relating to tuning set size, the number of decoder iterations, and k-list sampling. There were generally small differences relating to these parameters, however, indicating that the suggested approach is robust. The interaction between parameters does need to be better explored in future work, and we also want to explore better sampling, without duplicate translations.

This is the first attempt of describing and experimentally investigating feature weight optimization for direct document-level decoding. While we show the feasibility of extending sentence-level optimization to the document level, there is still much more work to be done. We would, for instance, like to investigate other optimization procedures, especially for systems with a high number of features. Most importantly, there is a large need for the development of useful discourse-level features for SMT, which can now be optimized.

Acknowledgments

This work was supported by the Swedish strategic research programme eSSENCE.

References

Chris Callison-Burch, Philipp Koehn, Christof Monz, Matt Post, Radu Soricut, and Lucia Specia. 2012. Findings of the 2012 workshop on statistical machine translation. In *Proceedings of the Seventh Workshop on Statistical Machine Translation*, pages 10–51, Montréal, Canada.

Marine Carpuat and Dekai Wu. 2007. Improving statistical machine translation using word sense disambiguation. In *Proceedings of the 2007 Joint Conference on Empirical Methods in Natural Language Processing and Computational Natural Language Learning*, pages 61–72, Prague, Czech Republic.

Marine Carpuat. 2009. One translation per discourse. In *Proceedings of the Workshop on Semantic Evaluations: Recent Achievements and Future Directions (SEW-2009)*, pages 19–27, Boulder, Colorado.

Yee Seng Chan, Hwee Tou Ng, and David Chiang. 2007. Word sense disambiguation improves statistical machine translation. In *Proceedings of the 45th Annual Meeting of the ACL*, pages 33–40, Prague, Czech Republic.

Colin Cherry and George Foster. 2012. Batch tuning strategies for statistical machine translation. In *Proceedings of the 2012 Conference of the North American Chapter of the Association for Computational Linguistics: Human Language Technologies*, pages 427–436, Montréal, Canada.

David Chiang, Yuval Marton, and Philip Resnik. 2008. Online large-margin training of syntactic and structural translation features. In *Proceedings of Human Language Technologies: The 2008 Annual Conference of the NAACL*, pages 224–233, Honolulu, Hawaii.

Jonathan H. Clark, Chris Dyer, Alon Lavie, and Noah A. Smith. 2011. Better hypothesis testing for statistical machine translation: Controlling for optimizer instability. In *Proceedings of the 49th Annual Meeting of the ACL: Human Language Technologies*, pages 176–181, Portland, Oregon, USA.

Louise Deléger, Magnus Merkel, and Pierre Zweigenbaum. 2006. Enriching medical terminologies: an approach based on aligned corpora. In *International Congress of the European Federation for Medical Informatics*, pages 747–752, Maastricht, The Netherlands.

George Doddington. 2002. Automatic evaluation of machine translation quality using n-gram cooccurence statistics. In *Proceedings of the Second International Conference on Human Language Technology*, pages 228–231, San Diego, California, USA.

Kevin Gimpel and Noah A. Smith. 2012. Structured ramp loss minimization for machine translation. In *Proceedings of the 2012 Conference of the NAACL: Human Language Technologies*, pages 221–231, Montréal, Canada.

Zhengxian Gong, Min Zhang, and Guodong Zhou. 2011. Cache-based document-level statistical machine translation. In *Proceedings of the 2011 Conference on Empirical Methods in Natural Language Processing*, pages 909–919, Edinburgh, Scotland, UK.

Zhengxian Gong, Min Zhang, Chew Lim Tan, and Guodong Zhou. 2012. N-gram-based tense models for statistical machine translation. In *Proceedings of the 2012 Joint Conference on Empirical Methods in Natural Language Processing and Computational Natural Language Learning*, pages 276–285, Jeju Island, Korea.

Liane Guillou. 2012. Improving pronoun translation for statistical machine translation. In *Proceedings of the EACL 2012 Student Research Workshop*, pages 1–10, Avignon, France.

Christian Hardmeier and Marcello Federico. 2010. Modelling pronominal anaphora in statistical machine translation. In *Proceedings of the International Workshop on Spoken Language Translation*, pages 283–289, Paris, France.

Christian Hardmeier, Joakim Nivre, and Jörg Tiedemann. 2012. Document-wide decoding for phrase-based statistical machine translation. In *Proceedings of the 2012 Joint Conference on Empirical Methods in Natural Language Processing and Computational Natural Language Learning*, pages 1179–1190, Jeju Island, Korea.

Christian Hardmeier, Sara Stymne, Jörg Tiedemann, and Joakim Nivre. 2013. Docent: A document-level decoder for phrase-based statistical machine translation. In *Proceedings of the 51st Annual Meeting of the ACL, Demonstration session*, Sofia, Bulgaria.

Christian Hardmeier. 2012. Discourse in statistical machine translation: A survey and a case study. *Discours*, 11.

Basil Hatim and Ian Mason. 1990. *Discourse and the Translator*. Longman, London, UK.

Mark Hopkins and Jonathan May. 2011. Tuning as ranking. In *Proceedings of the 2011 Conference on Empirical Methods in Natural Language Processing*, pages 1352–1362, Edinburgh, Scotland.

Philipp Koehn and Barry Haddow. 2012. Towards effective use of training data in statistical machine translation. In *Proceedings of the Seventh Workshop on Statistical Machine Translation*, pages 317–321, Montréal, Canada.

Philipp Koehn, Franz Josef Och, and Daniel Marcu. 2003. Statistical phrase-based translation. In *Proceedings of the 2003 Human Language Technology Conference of the NAACL*, pages 48–54, Edmonton, Alberta, Canada.

Philipp Koehn, Hieu Hoang, Alexandra Birch, Chris Callison-Burch, Marcello Federico, Nicola Bertoldi, Brooke Cowan, Wade Shen, Christine Moran, Richard Zens, Chris Dyer, Ondrej Bojar, Alexandra Constantin, and Evan Herbst. 2007. Moses: Open source toolkit for statistical machine translation. In *Proceedings of the 45th Annual Meeting of the ACL, Demo and Poster Sessions*, pages 177–180, Prague, Czech Republic.

Philipp Koehn. 2005. Europarl: A parallel corpus for statistical machine translation. In *Proceedings of MT Summit X*, pages 79–86, Phuket, Thailand.

Ronan Le Nagard and Philipp Koehn. 2010. Aiding pronoun translation with co-reference resolution. In *Proceedings of the Joint Fifth Workshop on Statistical Machine Translation and MetricsMATR*, pages 252–261, Uppsala, Sweden.

Thomas Meyer and Andrei Popescu-Belis. 2012. Using sense-labeled discourse connectives for statistical machine translation. In *Proceedings of the Joint Workshop on Exploiting Synergies between Information Retrieval and Machine Translation (ESIRMT) and Hybrid Approaches to Machine Translation (HyTra)*, pages 129–138, Avignon, France.

Thomas Meyer, Andrei Popescu-Belis, Najeh Hajlaoui, and Andrea Gesmundo. 2012. Machine translation of labeled discourse connectives. In *Proceedings of the 10th Biennial Conference of the Association for Machine Translation in the Americas*, San Diego, California, USA.

Franz Josef Och, Nicola Ueffing, and Hermann Ney. 2001. An efficient A* search algorithm for Statistical Machine Translation. In *Proceedings of the ACL 2001 Workshop on Data-Driven Machine Translation*, pages 55–62, Toulouse, France.

Franz Josef Och. 2003. Minimum error rate training in statistical machine translation. In *Proceedings of the 42nd Annual Meeting of the ACL*, pages 160–167, Sapporo, Japan.

Kishore Papineni, Salim Roukos, Todd Ward, and Wei-Jing Zhu. 2002. BLEU: A method for automatic evaluation of machine translation. In *Proceedings of the 40th Annual Meeting of the ACL*, pages 311–318, Philadelphia, Pennsylvania, USA.

Lucia Specia, Baskaran Sankaran, and Maria das Graças Volpe Nunes. 2008. N-best reranking for the efficient integration of word sense disambiguation and statistical machine translation. In *Proceedings of the 9th International Conference on Intelligent Text Processing and Computational Linguistics (CICLING)*, pages 399–410, Haifa, Israel.

Sara Stymne, Jörg Tiedemann, Christian Hardmeier, and Joakim Nivre. 2013. Statistical machine translation with readability constraints. In *Proceedings of the 19th Nordic Conference on Computational Linguistics (NODALIDA'13)*, pages 375–386, Oslo, Norway.

Jinsong Su, Hua Wu, Haifeng Wang, Yidong Chen, Xiaodong Shi, Huailin Dong, and Qun Liu. 2012. Translation model adaptation for statistical machine translation with monolingual topic information. In *Proceedings of the 50th Annual Meeting of the ACL*, pages 459–468, Jeju Island, Korea.

Jörg Tiedemann. 2010. Context adaptation in statistical machine translation using models with exponentially decaying cache. In *Proceedings of the ACL 2010 Workshop on Domain Adaptation for Natural Language Processing (DANLP)*, pages 8–15, Uppsala, Sweden.

Marco Turchi, Tijl De Bie, Cyril Goutte, and Nello Cristianini. 2012. Learning to translate: A statistical and computational analysis. *Advances in Artificial Intelligence*, 2012. Article ID 484580.

Ferhan Ture, Douglas W. Oard, and Philip Resnik. 2012. Encouraging consistent translation choices. In *Proceedings of the 2012 Conference of the NAACL: Human Language Technologies*, pages 417–426, Montréal, Canada.

Tong Xiao, Jingbo Zhu, Shujie Yao, and Hao Zhang. 2011. Document-level consistency verification in machine translation. In *Proceedings of MT Summit XIII*, pages 131–138, Xiamen, China.

Bing Zhao and Eric P. Xing. 2010. HM-BiTAM: Bilingual topic exploration, word alignment,and translation. In *Advances in Neural Information Processing Systems 20 (NIPS)*, pages 1689–1696, Cambridge, Massachusetts, USA.

Author Index

Banchs, Rafael, 1
Beigman Klebanov, Beata, 27

Flor, Michael, 27

Grisot, Cristina, 33
Guillou, Liane, 10

Hardmeier, Christian, 60

Li, Haizhou, 1

Meyer, Thomas, 19, 33, 43

Nedoluzhko, Anna, 51
Nivre, Joakim, 60
Novak, Michal, 51

Poláková, Lucie, 43
Popescu-Belis, Andrei, 33

Stymne, Sara, 60

Tiedemann, Jörg, 60

Webber, Bonnie, 19
Williams, Jennifer, 1

Zabokrtsky, Zdenek, 51